PRIMER *on* LARGE-SCALE ASSESSMENTS *of* EDUCATIONAL ACHIEVEMENT

NATIONAL ASSESSMENTS OF EDUCATIONAL ACHIEVEMENT

PRIMER *on* LARGE-SCALE ASSESSMENTS *of* EDUCATIONAL ACHIEVEMENT

Marguerite Clarke and Diego Luna-Bazaldua

1 2 3 4 24 23 22 21

ISBN (paper): 978-1-4648-1659-8
ISBN (electronic): 978-1-4648-1660-4
DOI: 10.1596/978-1-4648-1659-8

Cover and interior design: Sergio Andres Moreno Tellez, GCS Creative Services, World Bank.

Library of Congress Control Number: 2021905407.

Contents

Boxes

Figures

Maps

Tables

Foreword

Large-scale assessments of educational achievement are critical for countries to monitor system-level learning outcomes and identify factors related to student achievement. When done well, the results can inform important changes in policies and classroom-level practices and can efficiently capture progress toward global learning goals, including the United Nations' Sustainable Development Goal for Education and the World Bank's Learning Poverty Targets.

In order to be effective, large-scale assessments of educational achievement require solid political and financial support, careful planning, precise implementation, strong technical capacity, and timely and clear reporting. Because of these complexities, policy makers, national assessment unit staff, and other stakeholders frequently have questions about how best to handle the different stages of the assessment process. This World Bank *Primer on Large-Scale Assessments of Educational Achievement* is a response to those important questions. In addition, the book describes a variety of national, regional, and international large-scale assessments, and it discusses the experiences of low-, middle-, and high-income countries in using the information generated by these assessments to improve quality and learning.

My hope is that this book contributes to stronger national assessment systems that in turn support stronger education systems. By guiding stakeholders on the technical and logistical aspects of large-scale assessments, it is hoped they can avoid some unnecessary pitfalls and focus more of their time and efforts on making better decisions with the results.

Better assessments and better data are essential to inform policy and intervention design. If countries do not know what and how much students are learning, they are flying blind. Data are essential for better decisions. And better decisions are needed to eliminate learning poverty and achieve improved learning and educational opportunities for all.

Jaime Saavedra
Global Director, Education
World Bank Group

Preface

Over the past 10 years, an increasing number of countries around the world have initiated national large-scale assessment programs or participated in international large-scale assessment exercises for the first time. For instance, Nepal started its national large-scale assessment program in 2011; Ukraine participated in the Organisation for Economic Co-operation and Development Programme for International Student Assessment for the first time in 2018. In the same period, new regional large-scale assessments have been implemented in some parts of the world. Other long-standing regional large-scale assessments have undergone significant content and methodological enhancements; Southeast Asia implemented its first regional large-scale assessment exercise in 2019, and the Programme d'Analyse des Systèmes Éducatifs de la CONFEMEN in francophone Africa completely overhauled its long-running regional assessment to enhance the comparability of the results across countries and over time.

All of these activities have allowed policy makers and other stakeholders to obtain a better sense of the status of their education systems and, in some cases, to better monitor learning progress. Countries have also used the information that these large-scale assessments have produced to make more informed decisions about how to improve their education systems.

The World Bank Learning Assessment Platform team has developed this *Primer on Large-Scale Assessments of Educational Achievement* to support these large-scale assessment efforts. It comes in response to the significant demand we see from World Bank staff and clients for a concise, easy-to-read introductory guide on the topic. Accordingly, the main intended audiences for this book are task teams and clients working on the design and implementation of large-scale assessments. The book draws on content from the World Bank *National Assessments of Educational Achievement* book series, which has served over the years as a valuable source of information on the design, implementation, and use of national and international large-scale assessments. At the same time, this new book goes beyond that series to answer questions about new trends in national and international large-scale assessments, and it provides new country examples and updated information on regional and international large-scale assessments over the past 10 years.

The nine chapters in the primer have been structured to address frequently asked questions from people working on large-scale assessment projects and those interested in making informed decisions about them.

- **Chapter 1** introduces the reader to key concepts about large-scale assessments and some of the factors driving their increased relevance for global and national decision making.

- **Chapter 2** covers the use of large-scale assessment findings for the improvement of national education systems.
- **Chapters 3 to 7** discuss critical aspects of planning and implementing large-scale assessments and of the analysis and dissemination of large-scale assessment results.
- **Chapters 8 and 9** review the main regional and international large-scale assessment programs.

Acknowledgments

Marguerite Clarke, Senior Education Specialist, and Diego Luna-Bazaldua, Education Specialist, developed this book. Shauna Sweet contributed a summary of key information from the *National Assessments of Educational Achievement* book series and updated examples. The team received support and inputs from Julia Liberman and Victoria Levin and worked under the overall guidance of Jaime Saavedra (Global Director, Education Global Practice), Omar Arias (Practice Manager, Education Global Knowledge and Innovation Team), and Cristian Aedo (Practice Manager, South Asia Education Team).

Peer reviewers included Melissa Ann Adelman, Laura Gregory, Emma Gremley (Foreign, Commonwealth and Development Office, United Kingdom), Rafael de Hoyos Navarro, Yoko Nagashima, and Colin Watson (Department of Education, United Kingdom). Additional valuable inputs were received from Enrique Alasino, Hanna Katriina Alasuutari, Luis Benveniste, Michael Crawford, Joao Pedro Wagner de Azevedo, Diana Goldemberg, Sachiko Kataoka, Victoria Levin, Julia Liberman, Karthika Radhakrishnan-Nair, Shahram Paksima, Janssen Teixeira, Simon Thacker, and other members of the Education Global Practice who participated in discussions.

The Russia Education Aid for Development Trust Fund (https://www.worldbank.org/en/programs/read), managed at the World Bank by Julia Liberman and Victoria Levin with the assistance of Restituto Jr. Mijares Cardenas and Lorelei Lacdao, generously sponsored publication of this book.

About the Authors

Marguerite Clarke is a Senior Education Specialist in the World Bank's Education Global Practice. She leads the World Bank's work on learning assessment and has more than 20 years of experience working with countries around the world to strengthen their assessment systems. Before joining the Bank, she taught at universities in Australia and the United States; she also worked as an elementary and secondary school teacher in Ireland and Japan. She is former Chair of the Global Alliance to Monitor Learning Task Force on Sustainable Development Goal 4.1. She holds a PhD in educational research, measurement, and evaluation from Boston College.

Diego Luna-Bazaldua is an Education Specialist in the Education Global Practice, where he supports World Bank staff and clients in building capacity in the development of psychological and educational assessments. Before joining the World Bank, he taught at universities in Mexico and the United States. He also worked in the university entrance examinations department of the National Autonomous University of Mexico. He holds undergraduate and graduate degrees in psychology and statistics from the National Autonomous University of Mexico and a PhD in measurement and evaluation from Teachers College, Columbia University.

Abbreviations

CLA	citizen-led assessment
CONFEMEN	Conférence des Ministres de l'Éducation des Etats et Gouvernements de la Francophonie
EGMA	Early Grade Mathematics Assessment
EGRA	Early Grade Reading Assessment
EQAP	Educational Quality and Assessment Programme
ETEC	Education and Training Evaluation Committee (Saudi Arabia)
HCP	Human Capital Project
LLECE	Laboratoria Latinoamericano de Evaluación de la Calidad de la Educación
MES	Malaysian Examinations Syndicate
MoE	Ministry of Education
NAEA	National Assessment of Educational Achievement
NSC	national steering committee
OECD	Organisation for Economic Co-operation and Development
OREALC	Oficina Regional de Educación para América Latina y el Caribe
PASEC	Programme d'Analyse des Systèmes Éducatifs de la CONFEMEN
PILNA	Pacific Islands Literacy and Numeracy Assessment
PIRLS	Progress in International Reading Literacy Study
PISA	Progamme for International Student Assessment
SACMEQ	Southern and Eastern Africa Consortium for Monitoring Educational Quality
SDGs	Sustainable Development Goals
SEAMEO	Southeast Asian Ministers of Education Organization
SEA-PLM	Southeast Asia Primary Learning Metric
TIMSS	Trends in International Mathematics and Science Study
UNESCO	United Nations Educational, Scientific, and Cultural Organization

Chapter 1
INTRODUCTION AND OVERVIEW

Why Does Assessment Matter?

Building a strong education system that promotes learning for all is fundamental to a country's development and economic growth. The *World Development Report 2018* highlighted the learning crisis gripping many countries around the world and the central role of strong education systems in addressing that crisis. The report outlined three complementary strategies for moving an education system toward learning (World Bank 2018, p. 16):

- *Assess learning to make it a serious goal:* Measure and track learning better; use the assessment results to guide action.
- *Act on evidence to make schools work for all learners:* Use evidence to guide innovation and improve practice.
- *Align actors to make the whole system work for learning:* Address technical and political barriers to widespread learning.

This primer relates to the first of these strategies to promote learning. It describes how to design, develop, implement, and analyze data from large-scale assessments of educational achievement to help education systems highlight learning and improve learning outcomes. It also offers examples of national, regional, and international large-scale assessments that are being used to monitor and support learning in education systems around the world.

At its simplest, assessment is the process of gathering and evaluating information on what students know, understand, and can do (Clarke 2012). Decisions based on assessment results can vary from identifying the next steps in instruction for an individual student, to determining which applicants should be admitted to university, to designing systemwide policies and programs to improve teaching and learning in all schools.

Most education systems use three main types of assessment activities that correspond to three main information needs or purposes (annex 1A):

- *Classroom assessments* for providing real-time information to teachers and students to support teaching and learning in individual classrooms
- *High-stakes examinations* (also referred to as public or external examinations) for making decisions about the formal progression of students through the education system, for example, student certification, graduation, or selection decisions
- *Large-scale assessments* for providing information on overall performance levels and trends in the education system as an aid to policy decision-making.

Each of these assessment activities generates valuable information that can support the education process and thereby contribute to learning for all (box 1.1). For example, formative assessments by teachers in classrooms help to guide day-to-day instruction and tailor teaching to the needs of individual students. Examinations provide a standardized way to make merit-based decisions about the allocation of scarce educational opportunities among students. National and subnational large-scale assessments provide system-level insights and data on achievement trends that help guide systemwide reforms. The extent to which each of these assessments fulfills its purpose depends to a large extent on the technical quality of the instruments or processes used to determine what students know and can do, the degree of alignment between the assessment and the desired learning outcomes for the education system, and the effective education of stakeholders to understand and use the assessment results (Clarke 2012).

The World Bank has developed many resources to support countries in creating strong assessment systems that make effective use of each assessment type. This primer provides additional information on the topic of large-scale assessments. Additional resources for classroom assessments and high-stakes examinations can be accessed through the links provided at the end of this chapter.

BOX 1.1. A Quick Approach to Distinguishing among the Three Assessment Types

One way to differentiate between the three types of assessment activities is that classroom assessment is mainly about assessment "as" or "for" learning. Because of this, these assessments are primarily formative in nature. Alternatively, high-stakes examinations and large-scale assessments are mainly about the assessment "of" learning. As a result, they are primarily summative in nature.

What Are Large-Scale Assessments of Educational Achievement?

Large-scale assessments of educational achievement provide information on overall levels of student achievement in an education system for a particular curriculum area and at a particular age or grade level. Achievements of individual students are aggregated to estimate achievement levels in the student population as a whole at that age or grade level. This may be done by administering tests to a sample of students or to the entire population of students at that age or grade level. Teachers and other stakeholders (for example, principals and students) may be asked to provide background information, usually in questionnaires, which, when related to student achievement, can provide additional insights into how achievement is related to such factors as household characteristics, levels of teacher training, and availability of teaching and learning materials (box 1.2). The main audience for these large-scale assessments is typically policy makers; however, teacher trainers, curriculum developers, teachers, parents, students, researchers, and other stakeholders also use the information that these assessments produce.

Large-scale assessments around the world vary in several aspects, including the following:

- *School grades or age levels tested:* Most target students in primary or middle school grades.
- *Coverage of target population:* Most draw information from a representative sample of students and schools.
- *Subjects or skill areas covered:* Most assessments include language (or literacy) and mathematics (or numeracy), but other subjects or knowledge domains may also be covered.
- *Modality of administration:* Most assessments are paper based, but the movement to computer based and online assessments is increasing.
- *Background data gathered:* Most collect information on student home circumstances and teacher characteristics.
- *Frequency of administration:* Assessments are typically administered every two to five years.

Large-scale assessments also vary in how the results are reported and used. In most cases, results are used to inform low-stakes decisions about teacher policies and professional development, curriculum reform, and equitable allocation of resources to schools; in some cases, however, the results are used for high-stakes decision-making, such as imposing sanctions on schools that fail to meet performance standards or providing rewards to those that meet performance criteria. Research indicates that these high-stakes uses tend to have more negative than positive consequences for education systems and that the preferred approach is to use the results for lower-stakes purposes (Chung 2017).

Most large-scale assessments are national, measuring levels of student achievement in a particular country's education system. National large-scale assessments are usually closely aligned with a country's official learning goals,

BOX 1.2. Key Questions That Large-Scale Assessments Answer

All large-scale assessments seek answers to one or more of the following questions (Greaney and Kellaghan 2008):

- How well are students learning in this education system? Are they meeting specific learning standards?
- Are there particular strengths and weaknesses in student knowledge and skills?
- Do particular subgroups perform worse than others? Are there disparities, for example, between the performance of boys and girls, students in urban and rural locations, or students from different language groups?
- What factors are associated with student achievement? To what extent does achievement vary with the characteristics of the learning environment (for example, school resources or teacher preparation) or with students' home circumstances?
- Does student achievement change over time? What factors are linked to changes in student achievement over time?

standards, or curricula; they measure whether students in the system are acquiring the desired knowledge and skills described in the national curriculum. National assessments are implemented in many developing and developed countries around the world, such as Canada, Kenya, Kuwait, Nepal, Peru, Sweden, and Vietnam.

A variation on this approach is subnational large-scale assessments, which are confined to a region (province or state) within a country. They are common in federal systems (such as Argentina, Brazil, Canada, Pakistan, and the United States), where education is a devolved or concurrent responsibility and where a particular state or province may wish to conduct an assessment in line with its own learning standards, goals, and curricula. National assessments can provide a check on the quality of subnational assessments by flagging cases in which trends or levels of student achievement diverge between the two. In the United States, the National Assessment of Educational Progress has played this role.

Still other large-scale assessments are cross national. Cross-national assessments that involve countries in a geographic region, often with a common linguistic or cultural background, are referred to as *regional large-scale assessments*. Examples include the Programme d'Analyse des Systèmes Éducatifs de la CONFEMEN in francophone Africa and the Laboratorio Latinoamericano de Evaluación de la Calidad de la Educación in Latin America. (See chapter 9 for more information on these assessments.) Cross-national assessments that include countries from many regions are referred to as *international large-scale assessments*. The best-known international large-scale assessments are the Programme for International Student Assessment, the Progress in International Reading Literacy Study, and the Trends in International Mathematics and Science Study. (See chapter 8 for more information about these assessments.) International and regional assessments can provide a check on the information that emerges from national assessments.

Other large-scale assessments are more difficult to classify because they do not fit neatly into any of the conventional categories (see annex 1A). Two examples are the Early Grade Reading Assessment (EGRA) and the Early Grade Mathematics Assessment (EGMA).[1] EGRA was developed in 2006 as a simple, low-cost measure of pre- and early reading skills that governments, international development organizations, donors, or civil society could use in low-resource contexts (Gove and Cvelich 2011). EGMA followed a few years later as a measure of early mathematical or numeracy skills. EGRA tests letter recognition, phonemic awareness, ability to read simple words, and listening comprehension. EGMA tests number recognition, comparisons, and ordering sets of objects. Together, these two tools, and variations on them, have been administered in more than 50 countries and almost 100 languages. The EGRA toolkit provides a template that can be customized for a particular country using its alphabet, language, and texts. The EGMA toolkit is similar in nature.

EGRA and EGMA are meant to be administered orally to children (usually enrolled in grades 1 to 3) in a one-to-one setting. This individual administration can make the data collection exercise more time intensive than a typical large-scale assessment, which would be administered using paper and pencil or digital devices in a group setting. In addition, unlike most large-scale assessments, the results from an EGRA or EGMA exercise are typically reported in terms of student performance on individual items or tasks rather than as an overall score. EGRA and EGMA have functioned best to generate data quickly on reading and math levels in low-resource environments and as baseline and follow-up tools for impact evaluations of targeted interventions to improve early reading and mathematics. They also can be a starting point on the journey to creating more-standardized, more-representative, large-scale assessment programs aligned with a defined curriculum.

Another popular type of assessment is citizen-led assessment (CLA), which emerged in India in 2005 as a way to raise public awareness of low learning levels and to increase bottom-up accountability and action to improve the quality of education and learning.[2] Thousands of volunteers traveled to rural districts and administered simple reading and math tests to children at home. The dismal results helped stimulate debate and prioritize learning in national policy in India. From this beginning, CLAs quickly expanded around the globe and are now also used in Kenya, Mali, Senegal, Tanzania, and Uganda, among others. Many government-led, large-scale assessment programs could learn useful lessons from CLAs in terms of how to work effectively with the media to accessibly disseminate assessment results to the public. In general, CLAs are administered in people's homes, rather than in schools. As a result, they capture the learning levels not only of children attending school but also of those who have never enrolled or have dropped out. This approach is crucial to ensuring that no child is written off, particularly in countries with high dropout rates or where population subgroups are not enrolled in the education system at the same rate

1 https://www.eddataglobal.org/.

2 http://www.asercentre.org/.

as others. Unlike national large-scale assessments, the samples that CLAs use tend not to be nationally representative, and their content is not aligned with a specific national curriculum. In addition, given their lack of connection to the formal government system, there tends to be no direct link between CLA results and policy decisions.

Although most countries have a national large-scale assessment of educational achievement or participate in a cross-national large-scale assessment, not all do. Sometimes this is because of limited capacity; other times, however, it is because countries do not see the value of large-scale assessment studies. Table 1.1 lists some common arguments against implementing large-scale assessments and some possible responses.

In addition, some stakeholders do not see the value of the information obtained from large-scale assessment studies if they already have a high-stakes examination program. Therefore, it is particularly important to understand the differences between high-stakes examinations and large-scale assessments, because they provide very different kinds of information on student knowledge and are not interchangeable. Table 1.2 compares these two types of assessments.

TABLE 1.1. Common Arguments against Implementing Large-Scale Assessments

Argument	Response
It seems like a politically dangerous thing to do, particularly if the results show that achievement levels in the country are very low.	Well-constructed large-scale assessments can produce credible information on student learning and school performance, which—if presented in a way that makes the data relevant and understandable—can foster healthier political engagement and better education service delivery. The information also helps policy makers better manage a complex education system and make smarter decisions.
It only measures a very narrow range of the knowledge and skills taught in school.	Education systems have many goals, only some of which are captured by typical large-scale assessments of reading, mathematics, science, and social studies. It is understandable that stakeholders ask whether increasing the emphasis on measuring learning in these areas will crowd out the other goals, but a focus on measuring student achievement of core subjects and skills is more likely to "crowd in" these other desirable outcomes. Conditions that allow children to spend two or three years in school without learning to read a single word or to reach the end of primary school without learning to do two-digit subtraction are not conducive to reaching the higher goals of education.
It takes too much time to implement and achieve tangible results.	When well managed and planned, a national large-scale assessment exercise will take 12 to 18 months from conception to dissemination of results. International and regional large-scale assessments typically take three years from when a country signs up to when results are released. It is important to think about this investment as a long-term commitment to enhancing the quality and equity of education and learning outcomes in a country.
It costs too much.	Country savings from using assessment results to guide priorities and identify factors affecting educational outcomes exceed the costs of investing in these assessment systems (UNESCO 2016). Moreover, information about student achievement can support countries in developing programs to provide the skills that the labor market demands and in decreasing inefficiencies and inequities in their education systems.

Source: Original compilation for this publication.

TABLE 1.2. Differences between Large-Scale Assessments and High-Stakes Examinations

	Large-scale assessment	High-stakes examination
Purpose	Provide feedback on overall achievement levels to policy makers	Certify students or promote them to the next educational level
Frequency	Regular basis, for example, every four years	Annually and more often where the system allows for repeats
Duration	One or two days	One day to a few weeks
Who is tested?	Usually a sample of students at a particular grade or age level	All students at the examination grade level who decide to take part in the examination
Format	Usually multiple-choice and short-answer items	Usually essay and multiple-choice items
Stakes: importance for students, teachers, and others	Low	High
Coverage of curriculum	Generally confined to one to four subjects	Typically covers main subject areas
Effect on teaching	Little direct effect: Any effects typically happen through teacher professional development, curriculum reforms, or revisions to learning materials	Major effect: Teachers tend to teach what is on the examination; also tends to encourage extracurricular examination tutoring by teachers
Additional tutoring sought for students	Very unlikely	Frequently
Students receive individualized results	Seldom	Yes
Additional information collected from students	Frequently, in the form of student questionnaires	Seldom
Scoring	Usually involves statistically sophisticated techniques that permit generalization of results to target population	Usually simple process based on predetermined marking scheme
Effect on level of student attainment	Unlikely to have effect	Poor results or prospect of failure can lead to early dropout
Usefulness for monitoring trends in achievement levels over time	Appropriate if tests are designed with monitoring in mind	Not appropriate because examination questions and candidate populations change from year to year; furthermore, if examination is not aligned with national curriculum, results will not provide information on achievement of national learning goals

Source: Adapted from Greaney and Kellaghan 2008.

Countries with limited financial and human resources may be unsure about whether to conduct their own national large-scale assessment or participate in an international or regional large-scale assessment. Each choice has advantages and disadvantages (table 1.3). Countries need to decide what makes the most sense for them, given their context and information needs.

TABLE 1.3. Advantages and Disadvantages of National and International Large-Scale Assessments

	National		International	
	Advantages	**Disadvantages**	**Advantages**	**Disadvantages**
Benchmarking	Allows for benchmarking of student achievement against national curriculum goals and standards	No or limited information on how students would perform against peers in other countries	Allows for external benchmarking of student achievement against peers from other countries	Assessment may not be closely aligned with national curriculum goals and standards; results provide limited insights in those areas
Design and scheduling	A country can choose specific subjects, grade or age levels, and assessment timing and format that best suits its information needs	Tendency for assessment to be implemented on irregular schedule, with design variations affecting ability to track achievement levels over time	Design and scheduling clearly detailed, allowing countries to plan accordingly; scores from different administrations usually comparable over time	Design and scheduling may not always suit a country's policy and information needs; limited room to adjust assessment administration
Technical requirements	Technical requirements of assessment design can be matched to technical skills of national assessment team	Technical qualities of assessment may be poor, resulting in limited utility of the data	Opportunity for technical capacity building and exposure to innovative ideas and best practices in the field of large-scale assessment	National team needs some technical knowledge to fully benefit from capacity building
Data reporting and analysis	Data collected and reporting of results fully within country's control	Reporting of results tends to be delayed, making them less useful; databases may not be made publicly available, limiting opportunities for secondary data analysis	Opportunity to conduct extensive secondary analyses drawing on publicly available regional or global databases	National researchers need to be trained in how to use these very complex datasets

Source: Original compilation for this publication.

Why Are Large-Scale Assessments Important?

Over the past two decades, large-scale assessments of educational achievement have become increasingly important as tools to monitor and enhance the quality of education systems. Development of large-scale assessment capacity has enabled ministries of education to describe national levels of learning achievement, especially in key subject areas, and compare achievement levels of key subgroups (for example, boys and girls, urban and rural students, public and private school students). This information, in turn, has allowed governments to better direct resources to schools and students that need them. Large-scale assessments have also provided evidence to enable ministries to monitor whether standards of student achievement were rising or falling over time (Greaney and Kellaghan 2008). This information has been used as an input to policy decision-making and to evaluating the effect of policy reforms. Several global initiatives and trends have emphasized the importance of large-scale assessments in monitoring and promoting learning, including the following four:

- *Sustainable Development Goals:* In September 2015, 193 member states of the United Nations unanimously adopted the 2030 Agenda for Sustainable Development. Building on the Millennium Development Goals approved in 2000, the 2030 Agenda comprises 17 Sustainable Development Goals (SDGs), with the overall aim of reducing poverty and enhancing the lives of people around the world in a way that respects the climate and planet. The SDG for education aims to ensure inclusive, equitable, high-quality education and lifelong learning opportunities for all. The main indicator (4.1.1) being used to measure this outcome is "the proportion of children and young people (a) in grades 2/3; (b) at the end of primary; and (c) at the end of lower secondary achieving at least a minimum proficiency level in (i) reading and (ii) mathematics, by sex." To report on this indicator, countries must conduct their own national large-scale assessment or participate in a regional or international large-scale assessment. Because countries must continue to report on their progress leading up to the 2030 deadline, they must commit to a regular schedule of system-level assessment by investing in strong national assessment programs that can produce temporally comparable data or committing to regular participation in a regional or international large-scale assessment.
- *Human Capital Project:* In recognition of the importance of human capital in achieving the SDGs, and economic and social development more generally, in 2018, the World Bank launched its Human Capital Project (HCP). (See the additional resources at the end of this chapter for more information about the HCP.) The HCP aims to create the political space for national leaders to prioritize transformational investments in health and education as key inputs to human capital development. A core element of the HCP is the Human Capital Index, a biennial measure of the contribution of health and education to the productivity of the next generation of workers in each country (World Bank 2019). The education component of the index relies heavily on large-scale assessment data to generate a measure of learning-adjusted years of school, which gauges the number of years of schooling that children are receiving based on the amount of learning they demonstrate. By tracking changes in expected learning-adjusted years of school, countries will be able to monitor their progress toward full schooling and full learning for every child and SDG 4 more generally. To be included in the index and use it to track progress over time, countries must have access to regular, system-level data on student learning levels.
- *Learning Poverty:* In low- and middle-income countries, the learning crisis means that deficits in education outcomes are a major contributor to human capital deficits. In 2019, as a way to spotlight this crisis, the World Bank introduced the concept of learning poverty, which means being unable to read and understand a short, age-appropriate text by age 10. The indicator focuses on reading because reading proficiency is an easily understood measure of learning, reading is a gateway to learning in every other area, and reading proficiency can serve as a proxy for foundational learning in other subjects. The indicator begins with the share of children

who have not achieved minimum reading proficiency (measured according to the results of a country's large-scale assessments of reading) and is adjusted according to the proportion of children who are out of school and are assumed not to be able to read proficiently. The data released in 2019 indicated that 53 percent of children in low- and middle-income countries could not read and understand a simple story by the end of primary school. In low-income countries, the level was as high as 80 percent. The World Bank launched an operational target to cut the learning poverty rate by at least half before 2030. In addition to a literacy policy package focused on promoting the acquisition of reading proficiency in primary school, World Bank support includes assistance in strengthening large-scale assessment programs to close data gaps and better monitor whether more students are learning to read with comprehension over time.

- *COVID-19:* Before the outbreak of the global coronavirus (COVID-19) pandemic in 2020, the world was already facing a learning crisis, as high levels of learning poverty evidenced. With the spread of COVID-19, education systems faced a new crisis, as more than 160 countries mandated some form of school closures, affecting at least 1.5 billion children and youth. Research shows that the pandemic could cause learning poverty to increase sharply. Learning losses could be especially large among the most disadvantaged children and youth. As countries gradually begin to reopen their schools, they will need to take stock of student learning levels. A crucial aspect of this will be using large-scale assessments to gauge overall learning levels and identify specific subgroups or locations that need additional support in addressing learning losses and promoting learning recovery. These targeted efforts will be essential, given that demands on scarce global and national resources are at historic highs and the need to use these limited resources in a cost-effective way is greater than ever.

What Will You Learn from This Primer?

This primer is meant to be a first-stop resource for those wanting to understand how to design, develop, administer, analyze, and use the results from large-scale assessments of educational achievement. Each chapter introduces a stage in the process and offers tips, country examples, and things to consider or avoid. The primer is best used in conjunction with the World Bank *National Assessments of Educational Achievement* book series. The five volumes in that series go into more technical detail on many of the topics introduced in this primer.

The nine chapters in this primer have been structured to answer questions that those working on large-scale assessment projects and those interested in making informed decisions about them frequently ask. This chapter has introduced some key concepts about large-scale assessments and their relevance. Chapter 2 covers the use of large-scale assessment findings. Chapters 3 to 7 discuss critical aspects of planning and implementing large-scale assessments and analysis and dissemination of large-scale assessment results. Chapters 8 and 9 review the main regional and international large-scale assessment programs.

Annex 1A. Overview of Assessment Types

TABLE 1A.1. Assessment Types and Their Key Differences

	Assessment					
	Classroom	**Examinations**	**National**	**International**	**Citizen led**	**EGRA and EGMA**
Purpose	Provide immediate feedback to inform classroom instruction	Select or certify students as they move from one level of education system to the next (or into the workforce)	Provide feedback on overall health of system at particular grade or age level(s)	Provide feedback on comparative performance of education system at particular grade or age level(s)	Report on foundational literacy and numeracy skills of children in household settings	Report on foundational literacy and numeracy skills of children in school or household settings
Frequency	Daily	Annually and more often where system allows for repeats	For individual subjects offered on regular basis (for example every one to five years)	For individual subjects offered on regular basis (for example every three to five years)	Varies	Usually one-off exercises; sometimes used as baseline and follow-up for specific interventions
Who is tested?	All students	All eligible students	Sample or census of students at particular grade or age level(s)	Sample of students at particular grade or age level(s)	In- and out-of-school children	Varies, typically students in grades 1 to 3
Format	Varies from observation to questioning to paper-and-pencil tests to student performance	Usually essay and multiple choice	Usually multiple choice and short answer	Usually multiple choice and short answer	Usually multiple choice and short answer questions administered one-to-one or included in household surveys	Oral, one-on-one administration of short-answer questions
Coverage of curriculum	All subject areas	Covers main subject areas	Generally confined to a few subjects	Generally confined to one to three subjects	Focused on foundational skills that may or may not be aligned with curriculum	Focused on foundational skills that may or may not be aligned with curriculum
Additional information collected from students?	Yes, as part of teaching process	Seldom	Frequently	Yes	Sometimes	Sometimes
Scoring	Usually informal and simple	Varies from simple to statistically sophisticated techniques	Varies from simple to statistically sophisticated techniques	Usually involves statistically sophisticated techniques	Varies from simple to statistically sophisticated techniques	Simple aggregation of number or percentage correct for individual items

Source: Adapted from Clarke 2012.

Note: EGMA = Early Grade Mathematics Assessment; EGRA = Early Grade Reading Assessment.

References

Chung, Pearl J. 2017. *The State of Accountability in the Education Sector of Republic of Korea. Background Paper for the 2017–18 Global Education Monitoring Report.* Paris: UNESCO.

Clarke, Marguerite. 2012. "What Matters Most For Student Assessment Systems: A Framework Paper." SABER—Systems Approach for Better Education Results series, Working Paper No. 1. World Bank, Washington, DC.

Gove, Amber, and Peter Cvelich. 2011. "Early Reading: Igniting Education for All. A Report by the Early Grade Learning Community of Practice, Revised Edition." Research Triangle Institute, Research Triangle Park, NC.

Greaney, Vincent, and Thomas Kellaghan. 2008. *Assessing National Achievement Levels in Education.* Washington, DC: World Bank.

UNESCO (United Nations Educational, Scientific, and Cultural Organization). 2016. "The Cost of Not Assessing Learning Outcomes." http://uis.unesco.org/sites/default/files/documents/the-cost-of-not-assessing-learning-outcomes-2016-en_0.pdf.

World Bank. 2018. *World Development Report 2018: Learning to Realize Education's Promise.* Washington, DC: World Bank Group.

World Bank. 2019. *World Development Report 2019: The Changing Nature of Work.* Washington, DC: World Bank Group.

Additional Resources

- Education Home Page: https://www.worldbank.org/en/topic/education.
- Human Capital Project: https://www.worldbank.org/en/publication/human-capital.
- Learning Assessment Platform: https://www.worldbank.org/en/topic/education/brief/learning-assessment-platform-leap.
- Learning Poverty: https://www.worldbank.org/en/topic/education/brief/learning-poverty.
- National Assessments of Educational Achievement series: https://openknowledge.worldbank.org/handle/10986/32461.
- Student Assessment for Policymakers and Practitioners: https://olc.worldbank.org/content/student-assessment-policymakers-and-practitioners.

Chapter 2 HOW ARE RESULTS FROM LARGE-SCALE ASSESSMENTS USED?

The objective of a large-scale assessment is to measure what students know, understand, and can do with respect to a curriculum, knowledge domain, or skill in a way that provides an estimate of achievement levels in the education system as a whole. The results should address stakeholder information needs about achievement levels overall and for specific subgroups, strengths and weaknesses in student knowledge and skills, and within- and between-school factors linked to achievement and learning. This chapter discusses factors affecting the use and nonuse of large-scale assessment results, and it provides examples of how findings from national and international large-scale assessments have been used to inform education policy.

What Factors Affect the Use and Nonuse of Large-Scale Assessment Findings?

Factors affecting use or nonuse of large-scale assessment results may be political, institutional, or technical. For instance, key stakeholders may question the results of a large-scale assessment because they do not trust the organization that conducted the assessment exercise or because they do not fully understand the implications of findings presented in a highly technical manner (Reimers 2003). In other cases, policy makers may ignore politically sensitive results or prevent them from becoming public. Moreover, many countries lack the institutional capacity or resources to act on findings from large-scale assessments, even though stakeholders acknowledge their importance. The degree to which the results from a large-scale assessment are likely to be used also depends on (a) the extent to which the assessment is aligned with other components of the education system, (b) whether the assessment is perceived as technically sound, and (c) whether the results have been widely disseminated and the underlying data made available. Six factors affecting the use of large-scale assessment findings are discussed in more detail below.

STAKEHOLDER INVOLVEMENT

To increase the acceptance of assessment results, relevant stakeholders—including teachers, head teachers, school principals, and district superintendents—should be invited to participate in each stage of the assessment process, from the planning phase to review and interpretation of the results. Assessment findings also need to be communicated clearly and effectively to stakeholders, which necessitates that findings be presented in a variety of suitable formats and that an effective strategy for dissemination be put in place. Upon receipt of assessment results, stakeholders must be provided with an opportunity to review and discuss the implications for their work and to determine how the findings can inform legislative or other changes to improve student learning (Kellaghan, Greaney, and Murray 2009).

The importance of stakeholder involvement is particularly important when the results reflect inequities in the education system. Results from large-scale assessments often provide valuable evidence of equity, efficiency, access, or quality problems in the broader education system that might go unnoticed without stakeholder engagement. Box 2.1 illustrates the importance of stakeholder involvement using contrasting examples from Latin America and New Zealand.

DOMAIN CLARITY AND COVERAGE

Large-scale assessments are more likely to provide useful information when the knowledge domain to be assessed is well defined and aligned with the national curriculum or learning standards. When the assessment content is aligned with relevant, representative elements of the curriculum, the learning outcomes being assessed can inform curriculum implementation and achievement of national learning objectives (box 2.2).

It is generally not feasible to cover every aspect of the curriculum in a single assessment instrument. To reach a compromise between adequate coverage and reasonable instrument length, assessment specialists can take advantage of a rotated booklet design, which allows the breadth of information collected on a specific knowledge domain to be increased without overburdening the students completing the assessment (box 2.3). The use of rotated booklet designs requires staff with advanced training in psychometrics and expertise in the computation of plausible values and other relevant statistics.

COLLECTION OF RELEVANT BACKGROUND INFORMATION

Large-scale assessments are more useful for informing policy decision-making when they collect information to help stakeholders understand why student performance varies: for example, student sociodemographic characteristics

BOX 2.1. Importance of Stakeholder Involvement: Latin America and New Zealand

Latin America

Ferrer and Arregui (2003) describe the consequences of weak stakeholder involvement in the development of the first regional large-scale assessment in Latin America in 1997. Countries taking part in Laboratorio Latinoamericano de Evaluación de la Calidad de la Educación (LLECE) selected a national coordinator to act as their representative to the regional organization in charge of the study. In many cases, national coordinators were heads of national assessment agencies or worked in a unit at the Ministry of Education focused on student assessment. Although curriculum specialists from their country supported some national coordinators, others were not supported because of internal conflicts between curriculum offices and national assessment agencies. Therefore, some curriculum departments were not represented during the content definition and development stages of the assessment, which led to uncertainty about the extent to which LLECE was sufficiently aligned with these countries' learning goals. Not surprisingly perhaps, key stakeholders in these countries questioned the validity and relevance of the results when they were released. In subsequent studies, the regional team in charge of LLECE promoted broader involvement and participation of different country specialists to avoid this situation.

New Zealand

The New Zealand government contracted planning and implementation of its national large-scale assessment, the National Education Monitoring Project, to the University of Otago from 1995 to 2010. During this time, the university held extensive consultations to understand the views of professional groups and the wider community. In addition, teachers were heavily involved in assessment design and administration, and in scoring student responses. As a result of this inclusive process, the assessment results motivated a national debate that was critical to promoting changes in teaching and learning processes at the school level (Flockton 2012).

BOX 2.2. Alignment of Large-Scale Assessment Content and the National Curriculum in Ghana

Ghana's National Educational Assessment for grades 4 and 6 focuses on mathematics and English. Grades 4 and 6 were chosen over earlier grades because the national curriculum and language-of-instruction policies specify that students fully transition to English as the language of instruction in grade 4. Accordingly, the results from these assessments would allow policy makers to test student competency in English at the point of transition and two years after it.

The assessment team behind the development of the National Educational Assessment used the national curriculum and related materials as a guide to designing the assessment blueprint and instruments. For instance, based on the topics covered in the national curriculum for grades 4 and 6, the mathematics tests cover basic operations, numbers, measurement, shape and space, and data and chance. Similarly, the grade 4 and 6 English assessments cover listening comprehension, grammar, and reading (Ministry of Education, Ghana Education Service, and National Education Assessment Unit 2016).

BOX 2.3. Domain Coverage Using a Rotated Booklet Design: Mexico

Mexico's experience with international and regional large-scale assessments (for example, Programme for International Student Assessment and Laboratorio Latinoamericano de Evaluación de la Calidad de la Educación) facilitated its use of a rotated booklet design in its Plan Nacional para la Evaluación de los Aprendizajes, its national large-scale assessment program (Instituto Nacional para la Evaluación de la Educación 2015). The rotated booklet design involved six test forms, each of which had 50 items. Each test form contained two versions that helped create links between the forms and allowed for greater coverage of the domain being assessed. Despite differences in content between the test forms, psychometric analyses allowed for student scores from different forms to be expressed on a single scale (table B2.3.1).

TABLE B2.3.1. Plan Nacional para la Evaluación de los Aprendizajes Rotated Booklet Design for Mathematics Assessment

Test form	Test version		Average score	Number of items
1	A	B	692.79	50
2	B	C	690.31	50
3	C	D	682.23	50
4	D	E	678.50	50
5	E	F	670.49	50
6	F	A	677.14	50

Source: Instituto Nacional para la Evaluación de la Educación 2015.

and attitudes to learning, classroom practices, teacher subject-matter knowledge, classroom and school resources, and school and community factors. Collecting information on factors linked to student achievement can suggest pathways for action and make assessment results more relevant to stakeholders (box 2.4).

International large-scale assessments such as the Programme for International Student Assessment (PISA), Trends in International Mathematics and Science Study (TIMSS), and Progress in International Reading Literacy Study (PIRLS) collect extensive background information from students, teachers, and schools. In the Philippines, this additional information allowed government officials to see clearly that socioeconomic status was strongly linked to student performance on PISA and that low-performing students were clustered in specific schools (OECD 2019b). In addition, cross-national analysis of the TIMSS results has revealed that having a supportive home environment for learning is related to better student performance on the grade 4 mathematics test (Mullis et al. 2016).

TECHNICALLY PROFICIENT STAFF

For stakeholders to trust and use assessment results, they must have confidence that the assessments were designed and implemented in a technically robust

BOX 2.4. Role of Background Information in the Lao People's Democratic Republic National Assessment

In the Lao People's Democratic Republic, the Research Institute for Educational Sciences—part of the Ministry of Education and Sports—has been responsible for conducting the country's national large-scale assessment since 2006. The Assessment of Student Learning Outcomes tested grade 5 student performance levels in 2006 and 2009 and grade 3 student performance levels in 2012 and 2017.

Because it targeted students in the early grades, the 2017 study focused on foundational literacy and mathematics. It also included context questionnaires for students, teachers, and principals to obtain additional information on factors that influence student achievement (Research Institute for Educational Sciences 2018).

The 2017 study had the following objectives:

- Assess student learning outcomes and determine whether students are meeting expected learning standards.
- Collect and analyze background information on factors that influence student outcomes.
- Disseminate findings to stakeholders to improve teaching and learning.

Background information gathered as part of this study enabled the identification of factors linked to student achievement, such as:

- On average, girls show higher achievement in literacy than boys. Girls and boys have similar levels of achievement in mathematics.
- As teachers achieve higher levels of education, their students tend to reach higher levels of achievement in mathematics.
- Students enrolled in schools with single-grade classrooms had greater achievement in literacy and numeracy than their peers in schools with multigrade classrooms.

way that reflects, to the extent possible, best practices in educational measurement and evaluation (AERA, APA, and NCME 2014).

As discussed in greater detail in the next chapter, specialists involved in each step of the assessment process (for example, design, implementation, analysis, report writing, and dissemination of findings) must be technically proficient in their area of responsibility.

- *Psychometricians* must be able to apply standards for appropriate test development, administration, analysis, and use to each stage of the assessment process. This includes ensuring that the assessment framework and test blueprint appropriately reflect the target domain, that only items with appropriate psychometric characteristics are included in the final version of the test, and that student responses are appropriately analyzed and interpreted.
- *Statisticians* must be able to design and implement an appropriate sampling strategy, construct analytic weights, and analyze and accurately summarize the results.

- *Item writers* must be subject matter experts in the domain to be measured and employ best practices for authoring item stems and response options or criteria for evaluating written responses.
- *Test administrators* must ensure that each session is timed and that all testing protocols are adhered to, that criteria for student participation are understood and followed, and that participation and nonparticipation in the assessment are tracked.
- *Communications strategists* must be able to construct clear, consistent messages to communicate key findings to a broad range of nontechnical stakeholders.

Having well-trained, technically proficient staff helps to ensure that the assessment will be administered following appropriate procedures and best practices. For instance, Indonesia invested in specialized training for staff who would be responsible for the design, development, and administration of their national large-scale assessment (box 2.5).

BOX 2.5. Investing in Technical Expertise in Indonesia

Stakeholders in Indonesia expressed interest in participating in the Programme for International Student Assessment and Trends in International Mathematics and Science Study as a way to gain experience and technical expertise that could be applied to their own national large-scale assessment program (Lockheed, Prokic-Breuer, and Shadrova 2015). In addition to participation in these international large-scale assessments, Indonesia invested in developing the technical capacity of its staff in psychometrics and educational evaluation. These specialists have since worked at Indonesia's Ministry of Education and Culture, managing the country's participation in these international assessments and the development of their own national large-scale assessments (Lockheed, Prokic-Breuer, and Shadrova 2015).

CLEAR, EFFECTIVE COMMUNICATION OF RESULTS

Analysis and use of large-scale assessment results do not take place in a vacuum. It is important to be aware of existing priorities, pressures, and constraints within the education system. Presentation and communication of assessment findings must be sensitive to these concerns and to the intended and unintended consequences of the assessment for students and other educational stakeholders (Kellaghan, Greaney, and Murray 2009).

Assessment results should be summarized in a general report and further analyzed in reports tailored to the information needs of specific stakeholder groups such as policy makers, education managers, teachers, and students. The various ways in which assessment results can be communicated will be discussed in more detail in chapter 7. Findings should be disseminated to each of these audiences in a timely fashion and using clear language that they can understand. Findings from a national large-scale assessment are more likely to be used if they provide a clear indication of the factors affecting different levels of achievement and are diagnostic of problems within the education system. Assessment findings are more likely to be used when teachers understand the practical implications of the results and how information about the performance of the broader education system is relevant to their local classroom and school context.

BOX 2.6. Communicating National Large-Scale Assessment Results in Peru

Peru's national large-scale assessment program comprises census- (Evaluación Censal de Estudiantes) and sample-based (Evaluación Muestral de Estudiantes) assessments that complement each other in terms of school grades and subjects assessed. The Evaluación Censal de Estudiantes measures achievement of core learning goals, whereas the Evaluación Muestral de Estudiantes assesses a broader set of curricular content. Peru's Ministry of Education publishes national reports summarizing results for both assessments; results are reported as scale scores and in terms of four achievement levels. Peru also develops tailored reports for each region in the country and grade- and subject-specific reports for various stakeholders (such as school leadership, teachers, parents, and parents of students with intellectual disabilities). Reports are produced in seven languages, given the country's ethnic diversity; technical reports and special reports are published on topics such as educational equity, early childhood education, and longitudinal student achievement trends. The country makes available materials such as news briefs, policy briefs, videoconferences, and infographics that explain the uses and interpretation of their national assessment results (Ministerio de Educación 2019).

Box 2.6 describes the wide array of reports that Peru's Ministry of Education produced to inform various stakeholder groups about the results of its national large-scale assessments.

TRANSPARENCY AND FACILITATION OF ADDITIONAL ANALYSES

To fully use the information gathered, effort should be made to support analyses beyond the main findings and core summary for stakeholders. For example, assessment frameworks and data files from international large-scale assessments are publicly available on the internet for anyone interested in analyzing the data. Public access to this information allowed Liu, Wilson, and Paek (2008) to compare gender differences on the PISA 2003 mathematics assessment in the United States; their in-depth analyses revealed small differences favoring boys over girls in the four domains that the test measures.

Reimers (2003) found that researchers have shaped the demand for large-scale assessments through research using assessment data that has revealed the relationship among socioeconomic factors, teaching practices, school characteristics, and student achievement. For instance, Murillo and Román (2011) found that greater availability of facilities (such as libraries, computer rooms, and laboratories) and resources (such as books in the library) in schools was related to better student performance on the Latin American regional assessment.

Results of large-scale assessments can also be used as a starting point for other kinds of research studies. For instance, Kanjee and Moloi (2014) analyzed how teachers were using the results of South Africa's census-based Annual National Assessments in their classroom practice. The authors administered questionnaires and interviewed teachers to understand the possibilities and limitations in the use of national large-scale assessment data to improve teaching. The results showed that many teachers did not know how to use the Annual National Assessment findings and were not aware of any educational reforms or changes in school practices attributable to the results. The authors proposed some initiatives to increase teacher capacity and improve their skills for using the assessment data, including development of detailed performance descriptors to describe what students at different points along the scale know and can do, and pre-service and in-service teacher professional development programs on learning assessment.

What Are Some Common Policy Implications of Large-Scale Assessment Findings?

Well-designed and -implemented large-scale assessments can inform policy makers and motivate policies aimed at improving student learning in several ways. Findings from large-scale assessments can influence education policy by clearly defining the expected standards for student and education system performance, providing the basis for curriculum reforms, informing the reallocation or targeted provision of resources, guiding the modification of classroom practices, or supporting the development of policies or practices to strengthen community and school ties (Kellaghan, Greaney, and Murray 2009).

CLEARLY DEFINING EXPECTED STANDARDS

A country's national curriculum or learning standards outline what students at various levels of education are expected to know, understand, and be able to do. National large-scale assessments inform policy by operationalizing those learning expectations and measuring how well students are meeting them. The results may indicate that none, some, or all students are meeting these expectations in different subject areas and at different grade levels, which may lead to discussions on how to improve teaching, resources, or other factors to enhance student performance overall or for particular subgroups. Box 2.7 illustrates how Brazil has been using its national large-scale assessment results to monitor achievement of national learning goals.

International large-scale assessments provide the opportunity to compare standards across countries. Ertl (2006) describes how Germany introduced new national education standards after the PISA 2000 and 2003 studies. The results revealed poorer-than-expected performance and sizable achievement gaps between student groups. Factors such as student socioeconomic background and migration status partially explained student achievement in Germany. These findings motivated the introduction of new national education standards and performance criteria, with an emphasis on the expected competencies that all students should have acquired by the end of specific grades.

Similarly, Lockheed, Prokic-Breuer, and Shadrova (2015) note that international large-scale assessments have influenced learning standards in developing countries. For instance, after participating in PISA, the Kyrgyz Republic created new learning standards and improved the content and progression of its national curriculum.

BOX 2.7. Use of National Large-Scale Assessment Results to Monitor Learning Goals in Brazil

Brazil's national large-scale assessments include the census-based Avaliação Nacional do Rendimento Escolar and the sample-based Avaliação Nacional da Educação Básica. Together, these assessments cover students in grades 5, 9, and 12 enrolled in public and private schools. Both assessments measure knowledge and skills in Portuguese and mathematics; the Avaliação Nacional da Educação Básica tests additional subjects. Because these assessments cover the vast majority of students in the country and allow for results to be compared over time, the findings are used for system-level accountability.

For instance, the federal government has set national learning targets or goals that should be achieved within a specific time frame. Some of these goals are related to proficiency in Portuguese and mathematics by the time that students conclude high school. In line with this, the results of these assessments are used to generate national indicators linked to these learning goals and provide feedback to stakeholders about the education system's progress toward their achievement.

In the case of Portuguese, the learning goal states that "by 2022, 70% or more of the students will have learned what is appropriate for their age in Portuguese language." This goal is monitored using an indicator generated from results of the assessments, "Percentage of students in third year of high school with scores above the level considered appropriate according to the national assessments." In 2017, 27 percent of students had scores above the desired level, with an average annual increase of 0.49 percentage points, far from the goal set for 2022 (Paes de Barros et al. 2017).

International large-scale assessments also help set expectations for possible improvement trajectories over time relative to defined standards. PISA, TIMSS, and PIRLS all allow countries to track and compare changes in mean scores and proficiency profiles over time using advanced psychometric techniques. For instance, the PISA 2018 report showed trends in the proportion of low- and top-achieving students on the reading test between 2009 and 2018 (figure 2.1). These longitudinal comparisons reveal that Ireland; Macao SAR, China; Moldova; Qatar; the Russian Federation; and Slovenia have decreased the proportion of low-achieving students and increased the proportion of top performers over time (OECD 2019a).

PROVIDING THE BASIS FOR CURRICULUM REFORMS

A national large-scale assessment can provide a valuable conceptual framework and reference point for educators and policy makers with which the current curriculum can be compared and evaluated (Greaney and Kellaghan 2008). In the process of designing a national large-scale assessment, policy makers and curriculum development professionals may identify a gap between desired knowledge, skills, and abilities, and what is taught. A well-designed assessment instrument can in itself motivate curricular reform.

Student performance on large-scale assessments can inspire the development of new learning content and materials. An assessment may provide evidence that student achievement does not align with desired educational outcomes

FIGURE 2.1. Programme for International Student Assessment: Percentage of Low-Achieving Students and Top Performers in Reading, 2009 and 2018

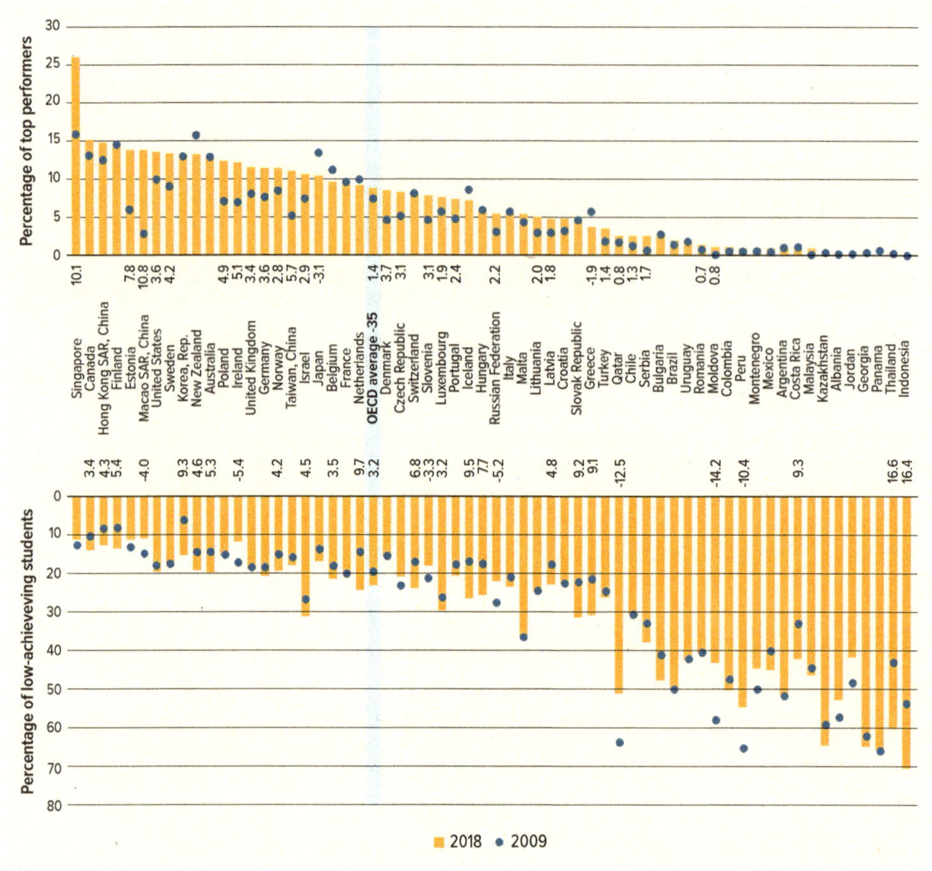

Source: OECD 2019a.

because of poor content coverage in one or more subjects (box 2.8). This may warrant a revision to textbooks or teaching manuals, as was the case in Jordan after its participation in TIMSS and PISA (box 2.9).

INFORMING RESOURCE ALLOCATION

One of the primary reasons for conducting a large-scale assessment is to understand how best to invest limited resources to have the greatest effect on education outcomes (Kellaghan, Greaney, and Murray 2009). For example, aggregated results from the 2007 administration of the Southern and Eastern Africa Consortium for Monitoring Educational Quality regional assessment revealed that only 61 percent of tested students had access to libraries in their classrooms or schools (Hungi et al. 2011), 42 percent had a reading textbook, and 41 percent had a mathematics textbook.

BOX 2.8. Educational Reform in Nepal Using the 2018 National Assessment of Student Achievement

Nepal has been conducting the National Assessment of Student Achievement since 2011, covering different school grades in each assessment round. In 2018, Nepali language and mathematics were assessed in grade 5; additional contextual questionnaires were provided to students, teachers, and head teachers from 1,400 schools nationwide.

Overall student performance on the National Assessment of Student Achievement reflected a lack of alignment between the intended national curriculum and the curriculum delivered in classrooms. Reports on the assessment recommended that the national curriculum, teaching methods, teacher motivation system, and learning environment be reviewed.

Assessment results also helped experts identify significant differences in student achievement according to province, district, socioeconomic status, gender, and school type. Other contextual factors associated with student performance included receiving feedback on homework, experiencing bullying in school, age and grade gaps, and participation in after-school activities. The experts recommended improving school physical infrastructure and distribution of resources, supporting initiatives to promote girls' education, and promoting additional co-curricular activities to support learning in community schools (Kafle, Acharya, and Acharya 2019).

BOX 2.9. Motivating Curricular Reform Using International Large-Scale Assessments in Jordan

With the intention of improving the quality of its education system, Jordan began participating in international large-scale assessments in the 1990s, implemented a review of the education systems of top-performing countries on the Trends in International Mathematics and Science Study and Programme for International Student Assessment, and went on study tours to these countries to learn about their education policies and practices. This comparative approach allowed Jordan to define appropriate benchmarks, implement best-practice changes to its national large-scale assessments, and propose strategic reforms focused on curriculum revision and teacher training programs (Abdul-Hamid, Abu-Lebdeh, and Patrinos 2011; Obeidat and Dawani 2014). Jordan broadened its national curriculum and linked it to the knowledge economy by defining a new skills framework that included academic skills, soft skills (such as communication skills), and personal management skills (such as responsibility and teamwork); the framework emphasized the need for the knowledge and skills taught in the new curriculum to be applicable to real-life situations (Obeidat and Dawani 2014).

Findings from large-scale assessments can influence the temporary or permanent allocation of resources across the system, within particular sectors, or between schools with characteristics associated with poor performance on the assessment. Popova, Evans, and Arancibia (2016) highlighted the relevance of resource provision in teacher training programs in developing countries in a systematic review of the effects of teacher training programs that found that providing teacher guides, textbooks, and other reading materials improved student outcomes on large-scale assessments.

FIGURE 2.2. Programme for International Student Assessment Trends in Colombia: 2006–18

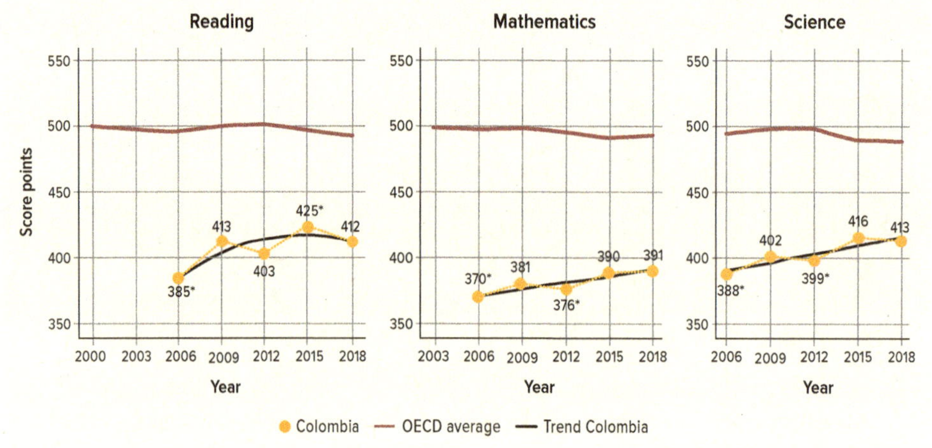

Source: OECD 2019c.
Note: * indicates mean-performance estimates that are statistically significantly above or below PISA 2018 estimates for Colombia. OECD = Organisation for Economic Co-operation and Development.

Assessment findings may also help direct resources to specific schools to address achievement gaps. For instance, since 2011, Colombia has implemented the Programa Todos a Aprender to improve learning outcomes of students in low-performing marginalized schools. The design of the program was based on results from Colombia's national large-scale assessment, Pruebas Saber (Instituto Colombiano para la Evaluación de la Educación 2019), and its participation in international large-scale assessments such as PISA. The main objective is to improve education quality measured according to language and mathematics scores by providing contextualized pedagogical materials, formative assessments, in-service teacher professional development and coaching, support to school leadership in school management activities, and improvements in school infrastructure (Diaz, Barreira, and Pinheiro 2015). Colombian student performance on PISA has improved since implementation of the program and other initiatives to improve educational quality and equity (figure 2.2).

GUIDING CLASSROOM PRACTICES AND TEACHER TRAINING

Results from large-scale assessments can also be used to guide changes in classroom practices and teacher training (box 2.10). For example, national large-scale assessments have helped identify deficiencies in teachers' subject-matter knowledge and shown a link between such deficiencies and lower student performance. Pre- and in-service teacher training can be mechanisms for addressing teachers' lack of subject-matter knowledge in critical domains.

Results from the 2014 Programme d'Analyse des Systèmes Éducatifs de la CONFEMEN [Conférence des Ministres de l'Éducation des États et Gouvernements de la Francophonie] revealed great variation in pre-service training of teachers in francophone African countries; for instance, 67 percent

BOX 2.10. Using Large-Scale Assessment Results to Provide Feedback for Classroom Practice in Argentina

Experiences in Latin American countries highlight the relevance of communicating large-scale assessment results to schools, teachers, and students. De Hoyos, Ganimian, and Holland (2019) found that providing diagnostic feedback on large-scale assessment results to teachers in Argentina resulted in greater student achievement than for students whose teachers did not receive diagnostic feedback.

When teachers receive diagnostic feedback on student performance, students report that their teachers devote more time to instruction and employ more learning activities in the classroom. Similarly, when teachers have access to diagnostic feedback, principals are more likely to use assessment results to make management-related decisions, including setting school-level learning goals, updating the curriculum, and make staffing decisions. Similar results highlighting the benefits of providing diagnostic feedback have been reported in interventions conducted in Mexico (De Hoyos, Garcia-Moreno, and Patrinos 2017).

of early primary teachers from Togo did not receive any pre-service training, whereas more than 72 percent of early primary teachers in Burundi had two or more years of pre-service training before working in schools (PASEC 2015). The assessment report also indicated that the most-experienced teachers tended to be assigned to the late primary grades, whereas less-experienced teachers started teaching in the early primary grades. Some countries have leveraged these assessment findings to support the development of better pre- or in-service teacher training programs or to inform better allocation of teachers to particular grades.

Using assessment results to improve teacher training is part of a broader education policy trend in terms of shifting away from an emphasis on inputs, measured by simply counting the number of trained teachers, and toward an emphasis on outputs, measured according to student learning outcomes. Countries with high achievement on international large-scale assessments are typically those that have invested in developing rigorous pre- and in-service teacher training programs backed by research evidence (Wei et al. 2009).

STRENGTHENING COMMUNITY AND CLASSROOM CONNECTIONS

Large-scale assessment results can reinforce the importance of family and community support as factors influencing student achievement. Policy makers may use these findings to inform strategies to strengthen links between classroom activities and student home life. For instance, results from the 2018 Pacific Islands Literacy and Numeracy Assessment showed that 50 percent of students reported that they never or only sometimes had someone at home checking or helping them with their homework. Policy makers may wish to act on such results to promote greater caregiver involvement in home-based student learning activities, given the positive association that has been found between such involvement and student achievement on the Pacific Islands Literacy and Numeracy Assessment and other large-scale assessments (Pacific Community Educational Quality and Assessment Programme 2019).

Key Ideas

- Stakeholders must be appropriately involved in large-scale assessment planning, design, and implementation, particularly when the results are likely to challenge current practices or policy.
- To be maximally informative for education policy and practice, the content of a large-scale assessment should be representative of target knowledge domains and learning outcomes.
- Collecting information on noncognitive factors (for example, sociodemographic, family, and school factors) linked to student achievement can inform changes in policy and practice to improve education outcomes and equity.
- Technically proficient, well-trained staff can help ensure that large-scale assessments are designed and administered in accordance with best practices, which, in turn, increases stakeholder confidence in the results.
- Large-scale assessment results should be disseminated in a timely fashion to stakeholders in language that they can understand and be presented in a way that is consistent with their information needs. Databases and technical information should be made available for secondary analyses.
- Findings from large-scale assessments commonly influence education policy by helping define education standards, motivating curricular reform, influencing resource allocation, setting and monitoring learning targets, modifying classroom practices and teacher training, and informing ways to improve connections between home and school to support student learning.

References

Abdul-Hamid, Husein, Khattab Abu-Lebdeh, and Harry Patrinos. 2011. "Assessment Testing Can Be Used to Inform Policy Decisions." Policy Research Working Papers, WPS5890. World Bank Group, Washington, DC. http://dx.doi.org/10.1596/1813-9450-5890.

AERA (American Educational Research Association), APA (American Psychological Association), and NCME (National Council on Measurement in Education). 2014. *Standards for Educational and Psychological Testing.* Washington, DC: AERA.

De Hoyos, Rafael, Alejandro J. Ganimian, and Peter A. Holland. 2019. *Teaching with the Test: Experimental Evidence on Diagnostic Feedback and Capacity-Building for Schools in Argentina.* Washington, DC: World Bank.

De Hoyos, Rafael, Vicente A. Garcia-Moreno, and Harry A. Patrinos. 2017. "The Impact of an Accountability Intervention with Diagnostic Feedback: Evidence from Mexico." *Economics of Education Review* 58: 123–40.

Diaz, Sandra, Carlos Barreira, and Maria del Rosario Pinheiro. 2015. "Evaluación del Programa Todos a Aprender: Resultados de la Evaluación de Contexto." *Revista de Estudios e Investigación en Psicología y Educación* 10 (10): 55–59.

Ertl, Hubert 2006. "Educational Standards and the Changing Discourse on Education: The Reception and Consequences of the PISA Study in Germany." *Oxford Review of Education* 32 (5): 619–34.

Ferrer, Guillermo, and Patricia Arregui. 2003. *Las Pruebas Internacionales de Aprendizaje en América Latina y su Impacto en la Calidad de la Educación: Criterios para Guiar Futuras Aplicaciones.* Lima, Peru: GRADE.

Flockton, Lester. 2012. *The Development of the Student Assessment System in New Zealand.* Washington, DC: World Bank Group.

Greaney, Vincent, and Thomas Kellaghan. 2008. *National Assessments of Educational Achievement, Volume 1: Assessing National Achievement Levels in Education.* Washington, DC: World Bank.

Hungi, Njora, Demus Makuwa, Kenneth Ross, Mioko Saito, Stephanie Dolata, Frank van Capelle, Laura Paviot, and Jocelyne Vellien. 2011. "SACMEQ III Project Results: Levels and Trends in School Resources among SACMEQ School Systems." http://www.sacmeq.org/sites/default/files/sacmeq/reports/sacmeq-iii/working-documents/levels_and_trends_in_school_resources_fin2.pdf.

Instituto Colombiano para la Evaluación de la Educación. 2019. "La Prueba Saber 3°, 5° y 9° en 2017. Los Resultados a Nivel Estudiante y los Factores Asociados al Aprendizaje." https://www.icfes.gov.co/edicion-28-boletin-saber-en-breve#https://www.icfes.gov.co/web/guest/saber-3-5-y-9.

Instituto Nacional para la Evaluación de la Educación. 2015. *Manual Técnico del Plan Nacional para la Evaluación de los Aprendizajes PLANEA 2015. Sexto de Primaria y Tercero de Secundaria.* México: Instituto Nacional para la Evaluación de la Educación.

Kafle, Badusev, Shyam Prasad Acharya, and Deviram Acharya. 2019. *National Assessment of Student Achievement 2018: Main Report.* Nepal: Education Review Office. http://www.ero.gov.np/article/303/nasa-report-2018.html.

Kanjee, Anil, and Qetelo Moloi. 2014. "South African Teachers' Use of National Assessment Data." *South African Journal of Childhood Education* 4 (2): 90–113.

Kellaghan, Thomas, Vincent Greaney, and Scott Murray. 2009. *National Assessments of Educational Achievement, Volume 5: Using the Results of a National Assessment of Educational Achievement*. Washington, DC: World Bank.

Liu, Ou Lydia, Mark Wilson, and Insu Paek. 2008. "A Multidimensional Rasch Analysis of Gender Differences in PISA Mathematics." *Journal of Applied Measurement* 9 (1): 18–35.

Lockheed, Marlaine, Tijana Prokic-Breuer, and Anna Shadrova. 2015. *The Experience of Middle-Income Countries Participating in PISA 2000–2015*. Washington, DC, and Paris, France: World Bank and OECD Publishing. doi:10.1787/9789264246195-en.

Ministerio de Educación. 2019. *Oficina de Medición de la Calidad de los Aprendizajes: Evaluación*. http://umc.minedu.gob.pe/ece2018/#1553619963598-f0a822b6-7323.

Ministry of Education, Ghana Education Service, and NAEU (National Education Assessment Unit). 2016. *Ghana 2016 Education Assessment. Report of Findings*. https://sapghana.com/data/documents/2016-NEA-Findings-Report_17Nov2016_Public-FINAL.pdf.

Mullis, Ina V. S., Michael O. Martin, Pierre Foy, and Martin Hooper. 2016. *TIMSS 2015 International Results in Mathematics*. Chestnut Hill, MA: TIMSS and PIRLS International Study Center. http://timssandpirls.bc.edu/timss2015/international-results/.

Murillo, Javier, and Marcela Román. 2011. "School Infrastructure and Resources Do Matter: Analysis of the Incidence of School Resources on the Performance of Latin American Students." *School Effectiveness and School Improvement* 22 (1): 29–50.

Obeidat, Osamha, and Zaina Dawani. 2014. *Disseminating and Using Student Assessment Information in Jordan*. Washington, DC: World Bank Group.

OECD (Organisation for Economic Co-operation and Development). 2019a. *PISA 2018 Results, Volume I. What Students Know and Can Do*. Paris, France: OECD Publishing. https://www.oecd.org/pisa/publications/pisa-2018-results-volume-i-5f07c754-en.htm.

OECD (Organisation for Economic Co-operation and Development). 2019b. *Results from PISA 2018. Country Note for the Philippines*. Paris, France: OECD Publishing. https://www.oecd.org/pisa/publications/PISA2018_CN_PHL.pdf.

OECD (Organisation for Economic Co-operation and Development). 2019c. *Results from PISA 2018. Country Note for Colombia*. Paris, France: OECD Publishing. https://www.oecd.org/pisa/publications/PISA2018_CN_COL.pdf.

Pacific Community Educational Quality and Assessment Programme. 2019. *Pacific Islands Literacy and Numeracy Assessment 2018: Regional Report*. https://research.acer.edu.au/ar_misc/31.

Paes de Barros, Ricardo, Mirela de Carvalho, Samuel Franco, Beatriz García, Ricardo Henriques, and Laura Machado. 2017. "Assessment of the Impact of the *Jovem de Futuro* Program on Learning." http://documents1.worldbank.org/curated/en/825101561723584640/pdf/Assessment-of-the-Impact-of-the-Jovem-de-Futuro-Program-on-Learning.pdf.

PASEC (Programme d'Analyse des Systèmes Éducatifs de la CONFEMEN). 2015. *Education System Performance in Francophone Sub-Saharan Africa. Competencies and Learning Factors in Primary Education*. Dakar, Senegal: PASEC.

Popova, Anna, David K. Evans, and Violeta Arancibia. 2016. "Training Teachers on the Job: What Works and How to Measure It." Policy Research Working Paper 7834. World Bank, Washington, DC. https://openknowledge.worldbank.org/bitstream/handle/10986/25150/Training0teach0nd0how0to0measure0it.pdf.

Reimers, Fernando 2003. "The Social Context of Educational Evaluation in Latin America." In *International Handbook of Educational Evaluation,* edited by T. Kellaghan and D. L. Stufflebeam, 441–64. Boston, MA: Kluwer Academic Publishers.

Research Institute for Educational Sciences. 2018. *National Assessment of Student Learning Outcomes (ASLO IV).* Vientiane, Lao People's Democratic Republic: Ministry of Education and Sports.

Wei, Ruth Chung, Linda Darling-Hammond, Alethea Andree, Nikole Richardson, and Stelios Orphanos. 2009. "Professional Learning in the Learning Profession: A Status Report on Teacher Development in the United States and Abroad." Dallas, TX: National Staff Development Council. http://edpolicy.stanford.edu.

Chapter 3
WHAT RESOURCES ARE NEEDED TO IMPLEMENT LARGE-SCALE ASSESSMENTS?

To ensure that findings from large-scale assessments are of sufficient quality to meet the information needs of stakeholders and support policy decision-making, assessment activities should be implemented in an appropriate institutional context, be adequately funded, and be undertaken by personnel possessing the necessary qualifications and expertise (Greaney and Kellaghan 2008). Although this chapter discusses these issues in the context of a national large-scale assessment exercise, many of the points are also relevant to other kinds of large-scale assessment exercises.

Who Is Involved in Planning a National Large-Scale Assessment?

MINISTRY OF EDUCATION

In most countries, the Ministry of Education (MoE) is directly involved in developing policies that support the national large-scale assessment program. It also tends to be a crucial source of funding for national large-scale assessment activities and plays an important role in decisions about the policy matters that the assessments address, how often assessments should be conducted, and the target populations to be assessed (Greaney and Kellaghan 2012).

Although the MoE establishes the overarching policy framework and guidelines for the national large-scale assessment, implementation is often the responsibility of an external agency. This can help ensure impartiality in implementation of the assessment and reporting of results. For example, a group within the Education and Training Evaluation Commission, which is separate from the MoE, develops and administers Saudi Arabia's National Assessment of Learning Outcomes (box 3.1). In some cases, implementation may be the responsibility of a technical unit within the MoE. Box 3.2 describes the relationship between Malaysia's MoE and the Malaysian Examination Syndicate, a technical unit in the MoE in charge of developing and implementing all national large-scale assessments and examinations in the country. Despite the differences in their institutional structures and overall scope of work, the Malaysian Examination Syndicate and Saudi Arabia's Education and Training Evaluation Commission have similar responsibilities in terms of the work they are supposed to perform in their country's national large-scale assessment program.

NATIONAL STEERING COMMITTEE

MoEs usually establish a national steering committee (NSC) to provide oversight, guidance, and feedback during the planning phase of a national large-scale assessment exercise and to ensure that design decisions support the stated goals and meet the information needs of key stakeholders. Committee members are expected

BOX 3.1. Saudi Arabia's Education and Training Evaluation Commission

In 2017, the organization formerly known as the Education Evaluation Authority became the Education and Training Evaluation Commission (ETEC). ETEC is in charge of the evaluation and accreditation of education and training programs in Saudi Arabia. It enjoys legal, financial, and administrative independence from the Ministry of Education and reports directly to the prime minister.

It has the authority to evaluate, measure, and accredit qualifications in the field of education and training for the public and private sectors and to increase their quality, efficiency, and contribution to the service of the economy and national development.

Core responsibilities of the ETEC are as follows:

- Set national standards for educational evaluation, training, and general education curricula
- Promote measurement and testing work and services in the education and training system
- Conduct evaluation and institutional accreditation in the education and training system
- License professionals and workers in education and training
- Evaluate the performance of educational and training institutions and programs ending with a qualification
- Use the results of education and training evaluations to raise their quality and their contribution to the service of the economy and national development
- Develop key indicators, advise and consult, provide research, and support innovation.

Source: Adapted from Education and Training Evaluation Commission 2020.

BOX 3.2. Malaysia's Ministry of Education and the Malaysian Examinations Syndicate

The Malaysian Examinations Syndicate (MES), a unit within the General Directorate of Education in the Ministry of Education created by law in 1956, plans, develops, and conducts national large-scale assessments and examinations.

The standardized assessments and examinations that MES implements include the following:

- Primary School Achievement Test (national large-scale assessment program)
- Malaysia Certificate of Education in Secondary School
- Malaysia Vocational Certificate in Secondary School
- Malaysia High School Certificate in Post-Secondary School
- Malaysia Higher Islamic Religious Certificate in Post-Secondary School

The assessments and examinations that MES develops are based on Malaysia's national curriculum and learning goals. MES also advises and supports teachers with professional development and materials for school-based assessments and develops guidelines and instructions for assessment administration.

Core responsibilities of the MES are as follows:

- Formulate educational testing and measurement policies based on the National Education Philosophy and curriculum goals
- Articulate specifications for educational testing and measurement, administration methods, reporting forms, and quality control tools
- Develop test and measurement tools and scoring methods to assess students based on the curriculum
- Coordinate, produce, print, and distribute assessment and examination materials
- Manage logistics of and conduct assessments and examinations
- Perform data entry and data cleaning tasks, review and calculate statistics, and report results
- Conduct research to improve the quality of testing and measurement of education and certification
- Administer auxiliary services and provide advice regarding educational assessments
- Administer assessments and examinations and enforce examination rules and guidelines.

Source: Adapted from Malaysia Ministry of Education 2020.

to establish priorities and ensure that the assessment maintains an appropriate focus aligned with its objectives and purpose. The appointment of an NSC also has symbolic importance, lending visibility and credibility to assessment activities in the eyes of key stakeholders, which influences stakeholder involvement and use of assessment results (Greaney and Kellaghan 2008).

In terms of size and representation, the NSC should find a balance; it should be large enough that the needs of key stakeholders are represented, but its size should not obstruct logistics and its costs should not prevent the committee from convening as needed. Committee membership typically includes representatives from the MoE; individuals who represent the interests of major ethnic, religious, or linguistic groups; and representatives of key stakeholder groups who are expected to act on assessment findings, such as teachers and curriculum development experts (Greaney and Kellaghan 2008).

University researchers and faculty members with expertise in educational assessment are often selected as members of the NSC. They bring a depth of experience and knowledge to conversations about assessment design and implementation and ensure that technical best practices are considered at all stages of the assessment process. In Chile, faculty members from Pontificia Universidad Católica de Chile and researchers associated with its educational measurement and assessment center have supported national and international large-scale assessment initiatives in the country and across Latin America. Faculty members and researchers provide specialized training, make technical recommendations on assessment, analyze assessment data, and produce technical assessment reports (box 3.3).

BOX 3.3. Role of Centro de Medición MIDE UC of the Pontificia Universidad Católica de Chile in Supporting National and International Large-Scale Assessment Initiatives

The Centro de Medición MIDE UC of the Pontificia Universidad Católica de Chile (MIDE UC) has participated in educational measurement and assessment projects in Chile and internationally. This specialized technical center provides training and research support to several assessment organizations and ministries of education across Latin America and the Caribbean. For instance, it offers the following:

- Consulting in the design of content standards and assessment frameworks
- Specialized training and workshops on assessment and psychometrics
- Development of assessment tools to measure learning
- Support on use of assessment findings for improvement of education systems.

MIDE UC and the Pontificia Universidad Católica de Chile have also supported Chile's long-term technical capacity by developing new graduate courses on methodology, psychometrics, and assessment. Graduate courses taught by experts have trained the next generation of assessment specialists that Chile needs to conduct this specialized work.

Because of its expertise in assessment and psychometrics, MIDE UC has been heavily involved in regional large-scale assessment initiatives, such as the Laboratorio Latinoamericano de Evaluación de la Calidad de la Educación.

Source: MIDE UC 2020.

NATIONAL ASSESSMENT TEAM

The NSC oversees and directs a team of professionals who design and administer the national large-scale assessment. Within the budgetary and policy parameters that the MoE and the NSC set, the national assessment team is typically charged with conducting the following assessment-related activities:

- Determining a sampling approach (census based or sample based)
- Identifying curriculum areas to be assessed
- Developing the assessment framework and items
- Piloting and finalizing assessment instruments
- Developing, piloting, and finalizing background questionnaires to accompany the assessment
- Determining methods to use for data collection
- Drafting reports and documents to communicate results
- Specifying how results will be disseminated to ensure that stakeholders can learn from and leverage results of assessment activities
- Developing a timetable for future assessments (for example, annual or biennial).

There is considerable variation in the composition of teams responsible for implementing national large-scale assessments. Acknowledging that there may be some legislative or procedural restrictions on who can implement such an assessment, the structure of the national assessment team primarily depends on the competence and perceived credibility of team members. The team may comprise MoE staff, university faculty, individuals from the research sector, and national or international consultants who provide specific technical assistance. Assessment team members must be perceived as credible, so selecting the right personnel may require compromise because those whom the MoE or NSC most trust may not be the most credible in the eyes of the public or other stakeholders (Greaney and Kellaghan 2012).

The following section describes the characteristics and responsibilities of key personnel who should be part of the assessment team. The reader is encouraged to review volumes 1 and 3 of the National Assessments of Educational Achievement book series for more information on the composition of national assessment teams (Greaney and Kellaghan 2008, 2012).

KEY PERSONNEL

At the head of the national large-scale assessment team is the *national coordinator*, who manages the overall assessment effort and ensures that the team adheres to the budget, schedule, and overall directions that the NSC establishes. The national coordinator also provides technical oversight and guidance for implementation of assessment activities. As such, he or she should have sufficient familiarity with educational measurement and the knowledge domains being assessed to provide advice and consent for critical decisions. As the primary liaison for the assessment team, NSC representatives, and stakeholders, the national coordinator should be someone who has credibility with stakeholders and the ability to navigate the political and technical challenges of the assessment process (Greaney and Kellaghan 2012).

Depending on the scope of the assessment and its timeline and budget, the NSC may appoint an *assistant national coordinator,* who should have a specialized background and experience in the technical aspects of assessment to support the work of the national coordinator. The assistant national coordinator's primary responsibility is managing the facets and processes of assessment development and implementation.

Regional coordinators may be included as members of teams responsible for conducting national large-scale assessments in larger education systems. Regional coordinators are the primary liaisons between the assessment teams and the participating local schools in their region. They frequently manage data collection, communications, training, and dissemination activities in that region.

Item writers develop new assessment items that align with stated learning objectives. Item writers should be able to identify common errors that students make and use these to write items that can determine what students know and can do in a particular curricular area. Teachers in the school grades and subject areas that the assessment targets are often recruited to write and review items. Teachers understand how learning objectives are taught in the classroom and have realistic expectations for student achievement. To the extent possible, the implementing assessment agency should recruit teachers whose classroom experiences represent the breadth of the experiences of the student population to be assessed.

Test developers analyze relevant curricular focus areas, help develop assessment frameworks and test blueprints, conduct test and item pilot studies, and coordinate item development and review work.

Assessment items must be clearly written and presented in a way that all students who participate in the assessment can easily understand. In many countries, there is considerable variation in the primary languages that students speak and the language of instruction in schools; in such situations, assessment instruments should be translated to reduce the influence of language barriers on student performance. Although it is challenging to ensure the exact equivalency of translated tools, it is the responsibility of *translators* to ensure that instructions and items are as equivalent and clear as possible. Translators also assist in developing test administration materials and assessment reports in different languages. It is important that translators have a high degree of competence in the languages involved to ensure that findings from a translated instrument are of sufficient quality to support policy decisions. Moreover, translators should have some familiarity with the content being translated. It is good practice to have a minimum of two translators per language.

The assessment team will also need *statisticians* and *psychometricians*. During the planning stages of an assessment, psychometricians are responsible for documenting validity evidence for items under development. Statisticians and psychometricians are also needed to analyze the data from pilot studies and support the selection of high-quality items based on their psychometric properties. Statisticians can support the development of robust sampling strategies to ensure that a representative sample of students is selected. Once the data are collected, these specialists can support data cleaning and file preparation, development of sampling weights, and data analysis and interpretation of findings.

Conducting a national large-scale assessment requires careful and conscientious data management. *Data managers* ensure the accuracy of the data collected during the assessment and manage the processing and cleaning of responses, correct coding of scored responses, and maintenance of test and questionnaire data. To accomplish this, a data manager may coordinate and supervise several *data recorders* responsible for quick, precise data entry. Data managers also ensure that master data files are clean, annotated, and appropriately labeled for future reference or analysis.

Graphic designers provide inputs for development of tests and report materials to ensure their professional appearance, design visual representations in test booklets and images that accompany test items, and design charts and graphs in stakeholder reports and other published materials.

Capable *test administrators* are critical to the success of national large-scale assessments. They must ensure that all students consistently adhere to testing protocols, teachers and staff are not present when tests are being administered, testing materials are given to and collected only from students who have been selected to complete the assessment, all instructions for completing the test are delivered clearly, students understand how to record their answers, time limits for tests are strictly followed, and students' work is their own.

The implementing agency is responsible for selecting the personnel responsible for test administration. Test administrators should have strong organizational skills and experience working in schools and be committed to following test protocols precisely. Test administrators are often graduate students, retired teachers, school inspectors, ministry officials, or current teachers or administrators from nonparticipating schools or schools in regions outside of the one being tested. To avoid the public perception of bias and minimize risks to the validity of the assessment results, teachers of students who are being tested are typically not selected as test administrators.

Item scorers, needed when test items require constructed responses and are not machine scorable, must have adequate background knowledge of the content being tested, in addition to receiving training on the scoring procedures specific to the assessment. Item scorers may have a variety of backgrounds and may be drawn from university students, examination board personnel, teachers, and MoE staff. They must be trained in the scoring criteria and procedures to be used for the open-ended items to minimize subjective bias and increase reliability of scores.

Finally, although not officially part of the assessment team, the *school liaison* is the school contact point for the national large-scale assessment team. The liaison helps ensure that school staff are aware that the assessment will take place in their school and coordinates any preparations and logistics to ensure the orderly administration of the assessment in the school.

In addition to the technical roles and specialized skills described in the preceding text and summarized in table 3.1, there are several other considerations when selecting personnel for the national large-scale assessment team. The team must be able to act as a cohesive unit, even though staff may be hired in only a part-time capacity, on a temporary basis, or as consultants. Team members

TABLE 3.1 Roles and Responsibilities of Key National Large-Scale Assessment Team Personnel

Role	Primary responsibility
National coordinator	Manage implementation of assessment activities, as guided by the national steering committee; may be assisted by assistant national coordinator, as needed
Assistant national coordinator	Manage and provide technical support to assessment development and implementation, as needed
Regional coordinator	Coordinate between the national team and participating local schools within the region
Item writer	Develop new items to measure proficiency against stated learning objectives
Test developer	Ensure that items are aligned with the assessment framework and test the blueprint
Translator	Ensure that test instructions and assessment items are as equivalent as possible across languages
Statistician	Develop sampling strategy and support analysis of assessment results by developing appropriate statistical weights
Psychometrician	Analyze item quality and support item selection in advance of implementation; support interpretation of findings for stakeholder reports
Data manager	Ensure accurate, appropriate labeling of data and labeling and organization of data files to support future and continued analysis
Data recorder	Perform data entry and quality control
Graphic design specialist	Design stimulus materials for inclusion in assessment and any charts, graphs, and illustrations used in stakeholder reports
Test administrator	Conduct assessment and ensure that everyone present adheres to testing protocols
Item scorer	Review and score open-ended constructed responses, as needed

Source: Original compilation for this publication.

must be flexible and responsive, especially when faced with technical and political challenges during implementation that must be navigated efficiently and effectively. Team members need to be able to operate with an appropriate degree of independence, particularly when the results of the assessment are unfavorable or potentially sensitive to stakeholders. Team members should be aware of, and demonstrate sensitivity to, local educational contexts in which learning is occurring; this awareness should be reflected in the instrument design, the data analysis process, and the reporting of results (Greaney and Kellaghan 2012).

Figure 3.1 shows the organizational chart for the national agency responsible for developing and administering Chile's national large-scale assessment (Sistema de Medición de la Calidad de la Educación). At the top of the chart is the agency's executive secretary, who reports to the NSC. The NSC has five members selected for their experience and knowledge of the Chilean education system and appointed by the minister of education. The agency has regional liaisons who oversee assessment activities and communications in each of Chile's five macrozonas or regions. The agency also has units in charge of administration, internal and external audits, and legal processes linked to the assessment process (Agencia de Calidad de la Educación 2020) and four work groups focused

FIGURE 3.1. Chile's National Assessment Agency Organizational Chart

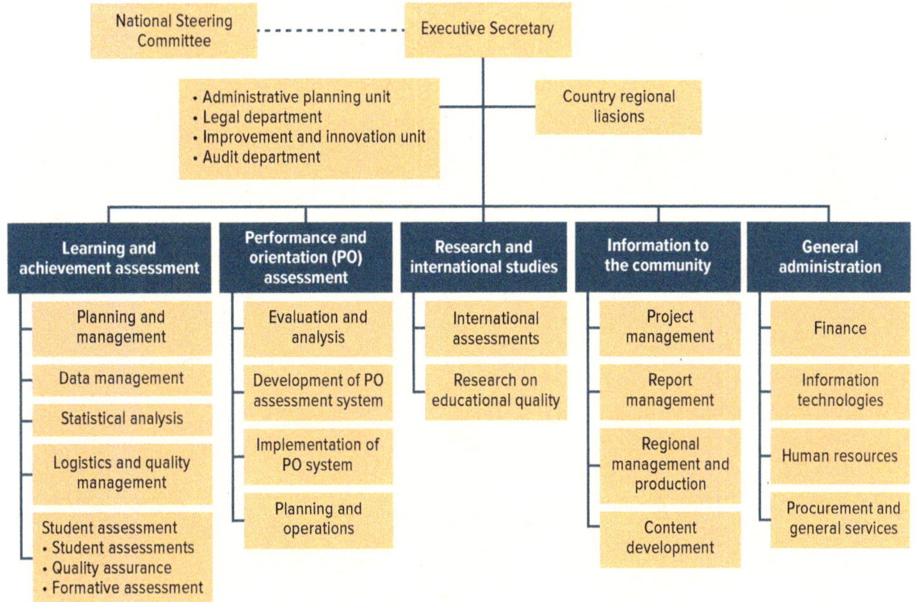

Source: Adapted from Agencia de Calidad de la Educación 2020.

on different aspects of student assessment. The Learning and Achievement Assessment group develops national assessments that provide information on achievement of national learning goals. The Performance and Orientation Assessment group supports self-evaluation capacities in schools. The Research and International Studies group oversees participation in international studies (for example, Laboratorio Latinoamericano de Evaluación de la Calidad de la Educación, Programme for International Student Assessment, and Trends in International Mathematics and Science Study) and produces reports about factors linked to educational achievement using data from national and international assessments. The Information to the Community group works with the other groups to develop national assessment reports and dissemination strategies. In addition, a General Administration unit provides cross-cutting support in finance, information technology, human resources, and procurement (Agencia de Calidad de la Educación 2020).

How Much Does a National Large-Scale Assessment Cost?

Developing a realistic budget and ensuring sufficient funding is critical to the success of a national large-scale assessment (box 3.4). Although there is no one-size-fits-all formula, table 3.2 includes a basic checklist of the main expense areas commonly associated with a national large-scale assessment. Because

BOX 3.4. Cost of Mexico's National Assessment as Percentage of Federal Budget for Education

Mexico's national assessment system has used census- and sample-based national large-scale assessments to monitor student achievement. The census-based assessment Evaluación Nacional de Logro Académico en Centros Educativos was administered from 2006 to 2013. From 2015 to 2018, it was replaced with the sample-based assessment Plan Nacional para la Evaluación de los Aprendizajes.

The civil organization Mexicanos Primero recently published an analysis comparing the total cost of these two assessments for 2008 to 2018, expressed as a percentage of the total budget allocated for education each fiscal year, adjusted for costs in 2005, which is taken as the baseline year before implementation of these national large-scale assessments. The census-based assessment accounted for, on average, 0.13 percent of the federal education budget, whereas the costs of the sample-based assessment accounted for 0.08 percent of the federal education budget (table B3.4.1).

TABLE B3.4.1. Comparison of Cost of Mexico's National Large-Scale Assessments, 2008–18

	Year	Total cost of national assessment (fixed to 2005)	Federal education budget	Percentage of federal education budget
		Mexican pesos (MXP)		
Evaluación Nacional de Logro Académico en Centros Educativos				
	2008	298,532,263	173,497,800,000	0.172
	2009	304,367,291	200,930,557,665	0.151
	2010	295,165,501	211,186,159,110	0.139
	2011	276,885,784	230,684,550,722	0.120
	2012	276,187,341	251,764,577,932	0.109
	2013	273,939,262	260,277,219,671	0.105
Plan Nacional para la Evaluación de los Aprendizajes				
	2015	368,402,163	305,057,143,549	0.120
	2016	123,409,468	302,986,555,681	0.040
	2017	166,505,446	267,655,185,221	0.062
	2018	235,317,375	280,969,302,366	0.083

Source: Gonzalez Seemann 2020.

TABLE 3.2. National Large-Scale Assessment Funding Checklist

	Source of funding		
Item	**Dedicated government funds**	**Other funds**	**Not funded**
Personnel			
Facilities and equipment			
Design of assessment framework			
Instrument design and development			
Training (such as item writing and data gathering)			
Translation			
Printing			
National steering committee			
Local travel to schools			
Data collection			
Data scoring (open-ended items)			
Data recording			
Data processing and cleaning			
Data analysis			
Report writing			
Printing of reports			
Press release and publicity			
Conference on results			
Consumables			
Communications			
Follow-on activities			

Source: Greaney and Kellaghan 2012.

circumstances will vary from country to country, some items may not be relevant for some national large-scale assessment programs.

The absolute and relative costs of assessment activities depend on a range of factors, including the scope of the assessment, item types, administration format (for example, paper and pencil versus computer based), and the number and types of schools selected to participate. The costs will also depend heavily on the local context, including available technology and fees associated with hiring personnel with specialized technical expertise (Greaney and Kellaghan 2012).

PLANNING AND DEVELOPMENT

Every assessment design decision has cost implications that should be carefully considered. In general, the more subjects and grades assessed, the more costly the assessment is. In addition, a census-based approach to data collection will, on average, cost more than a sample-based approach (Greaney and Kellaghan 2012).

Moreover, when new items are developed for the assessment, the budget must account for the training of item writers and the costs associated with pilot testing and item calibration procedures. Item scoring protocols and rubrics that will need to be developed for any constructed-response items also have costs involved. There may be costs associated with designing graphic or visual elements to be included in the assessment and printing answer sheets and other materials for paper-based assessments.

DATA COLLECTION

Data collection activities typically account for most of the cost associated with conducting a national large-scale assessment. Information must be collected from schools in advance of the assessment; assessment materials (such as test instruments, questionnaires, and manuals) must be printed, packaged, and delivered; test administrators may need to be trained on testing protocols and require support for travel or local accommodations; and completed test booklets and questionnaires must be collected. In each of these undertakings, the number of schools and students participating in the assessment is a direct determinant of cost. Assessment teams must also consider that the costs of conducting an assessment are likely to be greater in schools in remote areas (Greaney and Kellaghan 2012).

DATA PROCESSING

Once the assessment has been administered, test booklets and questionnaires must be processed and scored. The costs associated with these processes are frequently underestimated. Funding must be allocated for data entry and quality control and will depend on whether the tests are computer based or paper and pencil. Expenses for computer-based assessments include automatic scoring of student responses and use of data storage systems. For paper-and-pencil assessments, there are costs associated with scanning and machine scoring and scoring by hand for open-ended items (Greaney and Kellaghan 2012).

ANALYSIS AND REPORTING

Chapter 2 underscores the importance of producing multiple reports targeted to various stakeholder groups. Policy makers, teachers, and the general public are likely to benefit from differentiated approaches to reporting of assessment results to highlight their relevance for these diverse audiences. The cost of developing and disseminating these reports will depend on the number of reports, whether results are presented numerically or with narrative and graphical support, and whether the results are printed or made available electronically.

KEY PERSONNEL

Personnel costs associated with assessment activities will largely depend on whether the agency responsible for conducting the assessment has the necessary expertise. In some cases, assessment agencies may rely on consultants for specialized work that staff cannot perform. Consultants and advisers may need to be hired on a full-time or part-time basis, which will affect the project budget (Greaney and Kellaghan 2012).

MATERIALS AND FACILITIES

In addition to offices and facilities that full-time and part-time staff require, assessment organizations must have secure space for storing, organizing, and packing test materials before test administration and for processing test booklets and questionnaires upon completion of the assessment. The costs and resources needed to ensure secure storage of materials is often underestimated in budget calculations. There also should be common space for team meetings and coordination activities; staff will need access to office supplies, computers, and specialized software to support statistical analysis, graphic design, and report publication.

Key Ideas

- The value of the information collected through national large-scale assessments depends on the quality of design and implementation; assessment quality also requires that these activities be appropriately planned and resourced.
- The MoE establishes regulations and guidelines for national large-scale assessments and provides policy guidance to those who are developing and administering them.
- An NSC comprising technical experts and representatives of key stakeholder groups typically guides implementation; provides oversight, guidance, and feedback during the planning phase of an assessment; and ensures that design decisions support stated goals and meet information needs of key stakeholders.
- The national large-scale assessment team comprises a diverse group of technical experts who manage and conduct development and implementation activities.
- The money that countries save as a result of implementing changes to their educational systems based on national large-scale assessment findings exceeds the cost of investing in these assessments.

References

Agencia de Calidad de la Educación. 2020. "Diagrama de la Estructura Orgánica." https://www.agenciaeducacion.cl/nosotros/organigrama.

Education and Training Evaluation Commission. 2020. "About the Education and Training Evaluation Commission." https://www.etec.gov.sa/ar/About/Pages/default.aspx.

Gonzalez Seemann, Carlos. 2020. "Nota de Análisis. Evaluaciones de y para el Aprendizaje." https://s3-us-west-2.amazonaws.com/static-mexicanosprimero.org/2020/notatecnica/evaluaciones_de_y_para_el_aprendizaje_20201214.pdf.

Greaney, Vincent, and Thomas Kellaghan. 2008. *National Assessments of Educational Achievement, Volume 1: Assessing National Achievement Levels in Education.* Washington, DC: World Bank.

Greaney, Vincent, and Thomas Kellaghan. 2012. *National Assessments of Educational Achievement, Volume 3: Implementing a National Assessment of Educational Achievement.* Washington, DC: World Bank.

Malaysia Ministry of Education. 2020. "Lembaga Peperiksaan." https://www.moe.gov.my/korporat/bahagian-dan-unit/lembaga-peperiksaan.

MIDE UC (Centro de Medición de la Pontificia Universidad Católica de Chile). 2020. "About Us / An Overview." https://mideuc.cl/english/quienes.php.

Chapter 4
WHAT ARE THE KEY DECISIONS IN DESIGNING LARGE-SCALE ASSESSMENTS?

Every design decision that the national large-scale assessment team makes must be aligned with the stated objectives and planned uses of the assessment results. Once the reason for conducting a national large-scale assessment has been established, the national steering committee (NSC) is responsible for providing guidance on the who, what, and how of the assessment process: which students will be assessed, what competencies and skills will be assessed, and how students will demonstrate what they know and can do (Greaney and Kellaghan 2008). The national large-scale assessment team must work with stakeholders—including policy makers, teachers, school leaders, assessment experts, parents, and community leaders—to make the following key decisions:

- Which students will be assessed?
- Will the assessment be census based or sample based?
- How frequently will the assessment be administered?
- What content will the assessment cover?
- What item formats will be used?
- In which language(s) will the assessment be administered?
- Will the assessment include background questionnaires?
- How will the assessment be administered?
- What should be included in the test administration manual?
- How should students with special education needs be assessed?

- Does the assessment need to be adapted over time?
- What other technical considerations should be taken into account when planning the next large-scale assessment study?

Each of these decisions is addressed in this chapter. Although the answer to each one depends primarily on why the assessment is being conducted, all of the design decisions are interrelated. This chapter highlights some of these interdependencies, using examples from national, international, and regional large-scale assessments.

Which Students Will Be Assessed?

In many countries, policy makers are particularly interested in collecting information on student proficiency levels at crucial transition points in the education system. For instance, policy makers and other stakeholders may want to know about the reading levels of students who have just completed primary school and are moving to secondary school, or they may be interested in finding out more about the reading skills of those who have completed secondary school and are moving to higher education or who are entering the workforce. The specific ages or grades related to these transition points will vary from country to country. Depending on the country, the target population might be defined according to age, grade, or both. Defining the target population according to grade is recommended if there is considerable variability in the age at which students enter the formal education system (Greaney and Kellaghan 2008).

A country's education system may comprise many different types of schools (for example, public, private, charter, magnet, international, and vocational). Depending on the objectives of the assessment, the national large-scale assessment team may wish to assess students from some or all of these categories of schools. Most national large-scale assessments focus on assessing the achievement levels of students in regular public and private schools, which tend to include the vast majority of the student population.

Will the Assessment Be Census Based or Sample Based?

In a census-based assessment, all schools whose students meet the relevant age or grade criteria are required to participate. In a sample-based assessment, a subset of schools whose students meet the appropriate age or grade criteria are selected to participate; the participation of these schools in the assessment may or may not be mandatory (Greaney and Kellaghan 2008).

The choice of a census- versus sample-based approach depends on several factors, such as the intended use of the assessment results and the available budget (table 4.1). If the assessment will be used for school accountability or to provide formative feedback to schools in the form of report cards, a census-based approach is required. For instance, as part of their accountability policies, some countries use census-based assessment results to rank schools publicly and make decisions about them (such as resource allocation).

TABLE 4.1. Considerations for Sample- and Census-Based Assessments

Sample-based assessment	Census-based assessment
• Suited to low-stakes uses of results • Stakeholder need for information about overall education system rather than individual students or schools • More likely to require lower administration budget • Complete list of schools and characteristics available to construct representative sample • Technical support available for sample design and calculation of sample weights	• More likely to be linked to decisions about individual students, teachers, or schools that may be high stakes • Stakeholder need for information about all districts, schools, classrooms, or students in the system • More likely to require larger budget and more resources • Complete list of schools available

Source: Original compilation for this publication.

BOX 4.1. Sample-Based Assessment in the United States

The United States uses its sample-based National Assessment of Educational Progress to gain insights into the general status of school education across all US states and the District of Columbia. It is administered every year to a nationally representative sample of students in grades 4, 8, and 12. The sample is based on a multistage design, with students nested within schools and schools nested within states. The main subjects assessed are reading, writing, mathematics, and science; additional subjects assessed less regularly include civics, economics, geography, the arts, US history, and technology and engineering. The reading and mathematics assessments are administered every other year, allowing other school subjects to be assessed in the interim years. The assessment also includes background questionnaires for students, teachers, and schools. Results are reported for the nation and according to state and for different sociodemographic groups. Results for individual students and schools are not publicly available.

Source: NAEP 2019.

If the goal is to monitor the overall performance of the education system over time or to understand the contextual factors affecting learning, it may be more efficient to use a sample-based approach. Either approach can be used to inform continuous improvement and educational policy and practice.

When a national large-scale assessment is administered to a representative sample of schools, the results are meant to be generalizable to the overall target population in the education system (box 4.1), not to provide insights into specific sampled schools or the performance of individual students sampled for the assessment. Despite this limitation, a clear advantage of sample-based assessments over census-based assessments is the lower cost, which may be particularly relevant for developing countries with limited financial and human resources to administer student assessments (Wolff 2007).

Some countries, such as Chile and Brazil, combine census- and sample-based approaches in their national large-scale assessment design to more effectively meet stakeholder information needs. The combination helps reduce overall costs while providing a detailed picture of the education system (box 4.2).

BOX 4.2. Census- and Sample-Based Assessments: Chile and Brazil

Chile

Chile's national large-scale assessment, Sistema de Medición de la Calidad de la Educación, is administered annually to all students in grades 4 and 9 and biennially to all students in grades 6 and 8 (alternating the assessed grade each year). A sample-based approach is used to assess students in grades 2 and 10 (end of middle school) and to assess citizen education in grade 8. Chile's current combination of census- and sample-based assessments has allowed the country to reduce the number and cost of annual census-based assessments from their previous assessment design. At the same time, having a combination of sample- and census-based assessment has allowed Chile to introduce new large-scale assessments (for example, of citizen education) and new classroom formative assessments in the early grades.

Brazil

Brazil's national large-scale assessment system, Sistema Nacional de Avaliação da Educação Básica, comprises the Avaliação Nacional do Rendimento Escolar (also known as *Prova Brasil*) and the Avaliação Nacional da Educação Básica. Prova Brasil is a national census-based assessment of public school students in grades 5, 9, and 12. The Avaliação Nacional da Educação Básica complements Prova Brasil by assessing samples of public and private school students nationwide and covering a broader range of subjects and grades. Brazil uses this combination of sample- and census-based assessments to increase coverage of subjects evaluated in a wide range of schools (table B4.2.1).

TABLE B4.2.1. Brazil's Prova Brasil and Avaliação Nacional da Educação Básica

	Prova Brasil	Avaliação Nacional da Educação Básica
Participation	Census	Sample
School type	Public	Public and private
Grade levels	5, 9, 12	2, 5, 9, 12
Content area focus	• Portuguese • Mathematics	• Early literacy (grade 2) • Portuguese • Mathematics • Geography (grade 9) • History (grade 9) • Science (grade 9)

Brazil also has subnational large-scale assessments at the state level. Each Brazilian state has the autonomy to implement its own state-level assessments in addition to the Sistema Nacional de Avaliação da Educação Básica. To ensure the comparability of results among assessments, states and municipalities can draw common items from a national item bank and report scaled results at the federal level.

Source: Agencia de Calidad de la Educación 2020; Ministério da Educação 2020.

How Frequently Will the Assessment Be Administered?

Frequency of administration of a national large-scale assessment is commonly specified in the laws and rules that regulate the Ministry of Education and the national assessment agency. Because of the resources and logistics required for planning and implementation of a large-scale assessment, at least one year is required for each assessment round. Moreover, to facilitate more accurate comparison of assessment results over time, assessment agencies should plan the timing of each assessment administration—in terms of when it happens in the school year—well in advance and ensure that similar timing is followed in consecutive assessment rounds.

Some countries, such as the Republic of Korea, administer their national large-scale assessments every year. Others, such as Brazil (box 4.2) do so every other year. Still others have a less frequent schedule that may be more or less regular. For instance, Vietnam implemented national large-scale assessments in 2001, 2007, 2011, 2015, and 2019. The frequency with which countries administer their national large-scale assessments depends on a variety of factors, including available resources and information needs.

Frequency of regional and international large-scale assessment administration varies according to the assessment in question. Most regional and international large-scale assessment studies are administered every three to six years. Some regional large-scale assessments have less frequent study cycles depending on resources, logistics, and agreements with governments of participating countries.

What Content Will the Assessment Cover?

As discussed in chapter 2, assessment results tend to be more informative when assessment content is aligned with the national curriculum or national learning goals. This alignment is supported through the development of an assessment framework, which is a conceptual map of key learning outcomes for targeted knowledge domains, in conjunction with guidelines for how to measure the achievement of these outcomes. Curriculum documentation is often used to define knowledge domains and provide guidance on how students should demonstrate their knowledge, ability, or understanding of that domain in the context of an assessment. Curriculum and subject specialists can also judge the relevance and adequacy of the test content and its alignment with the national curriculum and national learning goals (Anderson and Morgan 2008).

Nepal's 2018 National Assessment of Student Achievement measured the achievement levels of grade 5 students in the Nepali language and mathematics (Kafle, Acharya, and Acharya 2019). The Nepali language assessment covered four broad domains of language use (listening, speaking, reading, writing) and grammar knowledge; the mathematics assessment included six general knowledge domains that students should have covered by grade 5 (box 4.3). These domains were chosen based on the national curriculum in each subject area. The assessment framework specified the number of hours of instruction devoted to each knowledge domain (as detailed in the national curriculum), which helped determine the number of items per domain to be included in the assessment.

BOX 4.3. Content Covered by Nepal's National Assessment of Student Achievement, Grade 5, Nepali Language and Mathematics Assessments, 2018

Nepali language	Mathematics
1. Listening	1. Geometry
2. Speaking	2. Numeracy
3. Reading	3. Arithmetic
4. Writing	4. Time, money, and measurement
5. Action grammar	5. Bills, budget, and statistics
	6. Sets and algebra

Source: Adapted from Kafle, Acharya, and Acharya 2019.

In addition to, or instead of, curricular outcomes, the NSC may wish to identify and prioritize other student learning outcomes aligned with stakeholder information needs. For example, countries may wish to measure the development of the broader skills that students will need after leaving school. In such cases, it may be more appropriate to focus on core foundational knowledge and transversal skills, such as problem solving and creativity, than specific elements of the school curriculum (Anderson and Morgan 2008).

When developing the assessment framework, national curriculum documents may or may not provide adequate definitions. As discussed in chapter 9, the global citizenship knowledge domain measured on the Southeast Asia Primary Learning Metrics (SEA-PLM) assessment was not in the national curriculum of any of the participating countries. In the absence of documented definitions, it is of critical importance that stakeholders agree on how these skills are defined and how they can be accurately measured. The same considerations apply to the measurement of student attitudes to learning and other socioemotional constructs; these attitudes also require precise, agreed-upon construct definitions so that they can be reliably measured and reported. Chapters 8 and 9 include examples of regional and international assessments that assess more innovative constructs.

What Item Formats Will Be Used?

Assessment instruments should use item formats that allow for the collection of valid, reliable evidence of student capabilities in relation to the knowledge domain or construct being assessed. In this way, well-designed assessments can reinforce curriculum intentions by modeling the skills and level of understanding that students should be able to demonstrate (figure 4.1 and figure 4.2).

Well-written items are critical in this process. Test items should, individually and together, provide valid, reliable evidence for what students know, understand, and can do. It is particularly important that items be aligned with the knowledge domains being assessed. All items must be developed following the specifications outlined in the assessment framework. Some item writing guidelines are listed in box 4.4.

FIGURE 4.1. Open-Ended Reading Literacy Item from Southeast Asia Primary Learning Metrics, 2019

	Afghanistan	Vietnam	Philippines	Nepal
Climate	Climate arid to semi-arid; freezing winters, hot summers	Tropical in south, monsoonal in north	Usually hot and humid	Subtropical in south, cool summers and severe winters in north
Geography	Landlocked and mountainous	Fertile Mekong river delta covers large part of south-western Vietnam	Made up of 7,107 islands	Landlocked; contains 8 of world's 10 highest peaks
Main crops	Wheat, fruits, nuts, wool, sheepskins	Paddy rice, coffee, rubber, cotton, fish	Sugarcane, coconuts, rice	Rice, corn, wheat, sugarcane, milk
Typical exports (goods sold to other countries)	Fruits and nuts, carpets, saffron	Crude oil, marine products, rice, coffee, rubber, garments	Electronic equipment, transport equipment, garments	Carpets, clothing, leather goods
Wildlife	Marco Polo sheep: has longest horns of any sheep	Saola (type of antelope): one of world's rarest mammals	Philippine eagle: largest eagle in the world	One-horned rhinoceros: world's fourth largest land mammal

According to the text, which country has the same exports as Vietnam?

____

Source: Adapted from UNICEF and SEAMEO 2017.

FIGURE 4.2. Example of Multiple-Choice Reading Literacy Item from Southeast Asia Primary Learning Metrics, 2019

The Hole

"I can see something shiny at the bottom," said Kit. "Maybe it's a gold coin."

"Don't be silly," said Sara, peering into the hole. Her younger brother was always seeing things, creating objects out of nothing.

"Maybe it's a sword," continued Kit. "Maybe a king buried a gold sword in the ground many years ago and then forgot about it."

"Maybe it's dirt, covered in dirt, covered in more dirt," said Sara. "It's just a hole, probably made by a wild animal."

"You are wrong!" exclaimed Kit. "No animal could make a hole as big as this!"

"Well, if you are so sure this is not an animal's hole, perhaps you should climb into it."

Kit began to turn pale. "Erm ... No. I cannot go in the hole ... because ... I have a sore foot!" Sara smiled; it had nothing to do with Kit's foot. A big hole could mean a big animal.

"I have an idea," she said, picking up a stone that lay beside her. "I will drop this into the hole. If we hear a clink, there is treasure. If we hear a thud, there is dirt. If we hear a yelp, there is an animal."

Sara dropped the stone and they heard nothing for a moment. Then they heard a splash.

Sara says, "I have an idea." What is her idea?

A) to push her brother into the hole.
B) to go into the hole to explore.
C) to throw a coin into the hole.
D) to drop a stone into the hole.

Source: Adapted from UNICEF and SEAMEO 2017.

BOX 4.4. Item Writing Guidelines

- Well-written items should:
  - Address a key learning area
  - Be a constructive, meaningful task
  - Be clearly mapped to a learning outcome, intended grade level, and cognitive process as defined in the assessment framework or test blueprint
  - Be fair and unbiased
  - Provide the student with clear direction on what they are required to do
  - Stand alone and not depend on understanding based on a previous item
  - Use simple, clear wording, avoiding vague, unfamiliar terms
  - Use short, direct, correctly punctuated sentences, avoiding difficult logic and double negatives
  - Be consistent in use of terms and measurements
  - Be culturally relevant and contextualized.
- Well-written multiple-choice items should also
  - Include response options of similar length and style. The correct answer should not stand out from the others because of its length, wording, or some other surface feature.
  - Include unambiguous response options. Avoid distractors that overlap in meaning.
  - Include only one correct response option. Avoid partially correct distractors.
  - Include plausible but incorrect response options.
- Well-written open-ended and constructed-response items should also have clear, objective scoring criteria.

Source: Adapted from Anderson and Morgan 2008.

Subject matter experts should be recruited to develop items. These experts are usually subject teachers who are experienced in the school grades assessed and curriculum specialists familiar with student learning trajectories. Teachers and other subject matter experts can also review and provide feedback on items that their peers develop. Training should be provided to teachers or other experts participating in the item development process who are not familiar with item writing and review procedures.

Most national and international large-scale assessments primarily rely on multiple-choice items to assess student achievement. However, it is often necessary to include short-answer, open-ended items as well, which require that students write a word, phrase, or sentence(s) to demonstrate understanding. Open-ended items are appropriate when the task can be accurately defined and reliably scored and a range of possible answers provide evidence of the targeted knowledge or ability (Anderson and Morgan 2008).

Figures 4.1 and 4.2 show open-ended and multiple-choice reading literacy items developed under the SEA-PLM assessment framework. As discussed in chapter 9, this regional large-scale assessment measures reading literacy using different text types (for example, narrative, descriptive, and persuasive) and drawing on different cognitive processes linked to reading comprehension (such as locating information in a text, interpreting information, and reflecting). The open-ended item in figure 4.1 requires the student to use reading skills to compare pieces of information about two countries. The multiple-choice item in figure 4.2 presents a narrative text and requires the student to locate information about the action that one of the characters takes.

In addition to the item development and content review process by subject matter experts, national large-scale assessment teams must pilot the items; the pilot helps determine the psychometric properties of each item and allows those with adequate levels of difficulty and discrimination to be selected. The pilot study is also a good opportunity to check for student understanding of each item in the assessment and address any content-related problems before the final assessment administration (box 4.5).

BOX 4.5. The Importance of Item Piloting

Before the final version of test booklets is constructed, it is important to pilot the proposed test items to identify those that provide the most accurate and reliable evidence on what students know and can do. A pilot should be conducted several months in advance of test administration to allow sufficient time for data collection and analysis and to create, print, and distribute the final version of the test.

The piloting process will help identify inappropriate items that should be omitted from the final version of the test, that may need revision before they can be included, and that are ready to be included in the final assessment. For instance, items that are extremely easy or extremely difficult for students at the target age or grade may need to be removed. Items that are unclear or have poor-quality distractors may improve if they are revised. It is also important to determine whether items perform similarly across population subgroups; no item should be systematically easier or more difficult for students of a particular sociodemographic group. If it is, it may need to be revised or removed from the final version of the test.

It is common to pilot two to three times as many items as will be included in the final version of the test. For instance, if the final instrument will include 30 items per subject, at least 60 items should be piloted for each subject. In addition to supporting the selection of items for the final test form, a well-designed pilot study provides the assessment team with an opportunity to improve the instructions for assessment administrators, determine the time it takes participants to answer the test items, identify student engagement during the assessment, strengthen scoring rubrics for open-ended items, and refine data collection procedures before test administration. Anderson and Morgan (2008) provide an in-depth description of how to plan for, design, and conduct a pilot.

Source: Adapted from Anderson and Morgan 2008.

In Which Language(s) Will the Assessment Be Administered?

National large-scale assessments are typically administered in the official language of instruction, but national assessment teams should be aware that the language of instruction may not be the language that students speak at home, which could become a barrier to assessing their knowledge and skills adequately, particularly in the case of younger students. In such instances, wording of test items may need to be simplified, or the test may need to be translated into students' home language. In addition, enumerators must be appropriately trained to administer the test orally in the language spoken in students' homes (Anderson and Morgan 2008).

Moreover, the intended language of instruction may not correspond to the language used in all classrooms, which has many potential implications for test design and administration. In those circumstances, the NSC will need to decide whether an alternative translated version of the test will be made available. Test translation and adaptation are time and resource intensive. It is critical to make the different translated versions of the test as equivalent as possible with respect to content and in terms of the psychometric properties of individual items and the instrument as a whole.

Will the Assessment Include a Background Questionnaire?

Research suggests that several factors can affect student achievement, and most national large-scale assessments collect information on these factors through questionnaires administered to students, teachers, and school leaders. Background information collected on students may include their gender, home language, educational history, home environment, classroom and social environments, and attitudes to learning. Questionnaires may be administered to teachers and school leaders to understand their pre- and in-service training, classroom experience, school management practices, and school and classroom resourcing (Anderson and Morgan 2008).

Table 4.2 summarizes the steps involved in developing background questionnaires, which are similar to those for developing assessment instruments. Given that national large-scale assessment teams are commonly operating with limited budgets, the additional information being collected through these questionnaires must support the objectives of the assessment; the focus should be on obtaining data relevant to factors that policy decisions can affect.

Furthermore, if these factors are intended to be used in complex analyses to explain variation in student performance, they must be well defined, and there must be evidence of their reliability and validity. Teams should also ensure that they have the necessary technical expertise to handle the complexity of the analyses required to use the data properly.

Table 4.3 summarizes some of the constructs that the school background questionnaire administered as part of the Republic of Korea's national large-scale assessment exercise covers (Ra, Kim, and Rhee 2019). The questionnaire gathers information about school characteristics, teachers' and principal's

TABLE 4.2. Components of Questionnaire Development

Component	Description
Purpose	Clarify purpose and potential use of questionnaire data
Blueprint	Design questionnaire blueprint to specify respondents, focus areas, item types, coding, and administration protocol
Items	Write questionnaire items
	Refine for clarity and usefulness in questionnaire panels
	Review questionnaires
Data and analysis	Specify plan for processing information, creating measurement variables and indicators, and conducting different types of analysis
Pretest	Design, produce, and proofread questionnaires for pretesting
	Write administration instructions for pretesting of questionnaires and train administrators
	Pretest questionnaires at same time tests are being pretested
Final questionnaire	Analyze pretest questionnaire data
	Refine questionnaire and administration instructions on basis of pretest data and feedback from pretest administrator
	Produce final form of questionnaire

Source: Adapted from Anderson and Morgan 2008.

TABLE 4.3. Example of Constructs That the School Background Questionnaire in the Republic of Korea's National Large-Scale Assessment Covers

Construct	Subconstruct	Variables
School finance	School finance	School finance
School principal characteristics	School principal	Principal's personal background Open hiring (that is, a recruited principal) Principal's activities
Student body composition and teacher characteristics	School size	Number of classes Number of students
	Student body composition	Student characteristics
	Teacher characteristics	Subject teacher training Teacher counselor training
Curriculum and school climate	Class and program	Ability grouping between classes After-school programs Student club activities Program for low performers
	School climate	Teacher climate Student climate Parent climate School management committee Parent school-event participation
	Use of results	Uses and interpretations of assessment results

Source: Adapted from Ra, Kim, and Rhee 2019.

background and professional training, school and classroom climate, and extracurricular activities available at the school, among other topics.

How Will the Assessment Be Administered?

Many international large-scale assessment programs offer paper- and computer-based administration; some countries have shifted to computer-based administration, but most still conduct their national large-scale assessment exercises using paper-based instruments. Countries may wish to consider computer-based administration because it presents several potential benefits, including the following:

- *Lower resource costs:* The time and resources required to print, package, and transport test materials for paper-based administration is significant.
- *Greater test security:* Paper-based administration requires that test booklets be labeled, collected, organized, and securely stored and transported; data from computer-based administrations are collected and securely stored digitally.
- *Greater reliability of results:* Computer-based assessments can be scored automatically for all multiple-choice items and some open-ended items. Scoring test booklets by hand using an answer key is likely to be less accurate and reliable than computerized scoring because of human error; scoring by hand is also much slower.
- *Greater efficiency:* Computer-based tests can be developed to be adaptive, meaning the test is dynamically created based on the student's answers. Computer adaptive tests typically take less time to administer and provide more precise estimates of student proficiency than nonadaptive tests.
- *Greater accessibility:* Computer-based assessments can be developed with accommodations that have the potential to increase test accessibility for students with visual impairments and other disabilities.

Significant barriers to implementing computer-based testing include the following:

- *Available infrastructure:* Participating schools must have the technical capacity to deliver the assessment. All students must have access to computers, and possibly a mouse and headphones, and that computer may need to be connected to the internet.
- *Test fairness:* Technology can affect students' computer-based test performance. When students do not have equal access to technology at school and at home, test scores may reflect differences in the technology literacy of students instead of differences in their knowledge of or ability in the target domain. At a minimum, administration procedures should provide students with time to familiarize themselves with the test format before beginning the assessment.

National large-scale assessment teams should consider several questions before moving forward with computer-based testing. For example,

- Are there target skills or abilities (for example, problem-solving or critical thinking skills) that are best tested using innovative item types available only through computer-based testing?
- Do participating schools have the information technology infrastructure needed to support administration of computer-based assessment?
- Do students have access to technology at school and at home?
- Do students have equal access to and familiarity with technology?

What Should Be Included in the Test Administration Manual?

The national large-scale assessment team must design procedures that ensure secure, standardized implementation of the assessment and that schools are aware of these procedures and their responsibilities during implementation. This information is communicated in the test administration manual.

Anderson and Morgan (2008) provide an overview of the contents of a test administration manual that includes the following:

- Test administrator tasks and responsibilities at each stage of the testing process
- Responsibilities of schools that participate in the assessment, including space requirements and room layouts for taking the test and special accommodations that the school must make for students who qualify for them
- Resources that test administrators must provide to students (such as test booklets and answer sheets, digital devices with assessment software)
- Resources that the school must provide to students (such as pencils, erasers, rulers, and calculators)
- School personnel other than the test administrator allowed to be present in the room at the time of testing
- Timing of the assessment—overall and for specific components
- Responsibilities that school personnel will have before, during, and after administration of the assessment.

In general, it is the school's responsibility to ensure the security of test materials, including appropriate storage space and any procedures that should be followed. Test and answer booklets should be appropriately marked with students' names or identification numbers and any other information needed to support data collection and analysis, such as the classroom, grade level, or school. Booklets should be checked against a complete list of students selected to participate in the assessment to ensure that all materials are collected after the test administration. Anderson and Morgan (2008) discuss how schools should handle tracking and adjust for students who do not participate because of unplanned or planned absences from testing. All completed test and answer booklets should be sorted and then stored in a locked room so that test materials cannot be accessed outside of designated testing sessions or by anyone who should not have access to those materials (Anderson and Morgan 2008).

How Should Students with Special Education Needs Be Assessed?

Ministries of education, national assessment agencies, and other organizations behind the development, administration, and use of large-scale assessments and high-stakes examinations are increasingly flagging challenges with assessment of students with special education needs. The professional standards for educational assessment highlight the importance of producing standardized assessments that facilitate accessibility for all students, as far as practicable. The assessment development process should adhere to the principles of universal design, which is based on the tenet that assessments must maximize accessibility and fairness for all students, irrespective of their personal characteristics (AERA, APA, and NCME 2014; ETS 2014).

Assessment teams should consider a variety of accommodations and adaptations for making assessments more accessible to students with special education needs. The specific accommodations or adaptions depend on the objective of the assessment, the knowledge domain measured, and the needs of specific groups or individual students (for example, physical, sensory, cognitive, and linguistic). These accommodations or adaptations should permit greater comparability of scores without affecting the validity or reliability of the assessment results. Effective accommodations or adaptations remove barriers to student performance without providing an unfair advantage over others who do not receive them (AERA, APA, and NCME 2014; ETS 2014).

Examples of some assessment accommodations include test forms in braille, large-print booklets and answer sheets, magnification devices for visual materials, read-aloud supports during the assessment, headphones or other audio devices, and extended time for assessment administration or multiple testing sessions.

Does the Assessment Need to Be Adapted over Time?

Each of the design decisions discussed in this chapter may need to be revisited with each assessment implementation. Stakeholders may have new questions about student learning that reflect emerging information needs; additionally, economic, social, or political factors may require changes from previous test administrations. It can take several years to establish a comprehensive large-scale assessment system and to implement an assessment that effectively and efficiently meets the needs of stakeholders (Anderson and Morgan 2008).

The Korea Institute for Curriculum and Evaluation, the student assessment agency of the Republic of Korea, has administered the annual National Assessment of Educational Achievement (NAEA) since 1998. The NAEA, which is based on Korea's national curriculum, is designed to capture trends in student achievement levels and school quality. Over the past 30 years, the Republic of Korea has implemented education reforms that NAEA results have informed and that have influenced the assessment's design (Ra, Kim, and Rhee 2019). The NAEA provides an important example of how the design of a large-scale assessment can adapt to the broader context over time and still be effective (box 4.6).

BOX 4.6. Republic of Korea's National Assessment of Educational Achievement Structure and Main Changes over Time

Formulation of National Assessment of Educational Achievement (NAEA) master plan (1998–2002)

- Master plan proposed assessment of two to three subjects per year.
- Assessment implementation started in 2000, including national samples of students at the end of elementary school (grade 6), middle school (grade 9), and the second year of high school (grade 12). NAEA eventually switched its focus from grade 12 to cover first-year high school students (grade 11).
- Assessment results were provided to students.

Methodological changes in NAEA (2003–06)

- Standard-setting procedures were used to define achievement levels.
- Common item designs were used to equate assessment scores and analyze achievement trends over time.
- Sampling design was systematized to increase generalization of assessment results.

Preparation for census-based assessment (2007–08)

- Before 2006, approximately 1 percent of students in assessed grades were sampled nationwide.
- The sample size increased to cover 3 percent of the student population by 2006. Further sample size increases to 4 percent and 5 percent were implemented in 2007 and 2008, respectively.

Census-based assessment (2009–12)

- NAEA became a census-based assessment in 2009.
- Assessment dates changed from October to July to cover the remedial education period of the school year.
- Assessment coverage changed from the first to the second year of high school.
- Information on school achievement was made publicly available.
- Individual assessment reports were provided to students, teachers, and parents.

Reduction of grades in census-based assessment (2013–16)

- Elementary schools no longer took part in census-based NAEA.
- Number of assessed subjects in middle school decreased from five (Korean language, mathematics, science, social studies, and English) to three (Korean language, mathematics, and English) in the census-based assessment.

Return to sample-based assessment (2017-present)

- NAEA became a sample-based assessment again covering middle and high school grades.

Source: Ra, Kim, and Rhee 2019.

What Other Technical Decisions Should Be Considered when Planning the Next Large-Scale Assessment Study?

Given ongoing advances in measurement, psychometrics, and technology, national and international large-scale assessments have become more technically complex and now include such features as rotated booklet designs (see section 2.1), plausible values, adaptive testing, and vertical and horizontal scaling. Table 4.4 summarizes some of the uses of these innovations in the context of large-scale assessments.

TABLE 4.4. Innovations and Their Use in Large-Scale Assessments

Innovation	Use
Rotated booklet design	Multiple test forms sharing a certain proportion of common items are produced to assess students in a specific subject and school grade. Rotated booklet designs increase the breadth of information collected on a specific knowledge domain without overburdening students and decrease the chances of test malpractice during test administration.
Plausible values	If multiple test forms are administered using rotated booklet designs, plausible values are used to report student scores on a common proficiency scale, even though they were not exposed to the same set of items.
Adaptive testing	Assessments are built on algorithms that permit administration of items at a level of difficulty aligned with a student's ability level. Adaptive testing requires availability of a large pool of items all expressed on the same difficulty scale.
Horizontal scaling	Statistical techniques are used to express student scores from different versions or administrations of a test (for example, different versions of a grade 5 reading assessment administered in two different years) on a common scale. The tests must share a proportion of common items. Horizontal scaling is commonly used to monitor changes in system achievement levels over time on a common scale.
Vertical scaling	Statistical techniques are used to express student scores from different tests on a common scale when students are in different school grades (for example, grades 5 and 8 reading assessments). The tests must share a proportion of common items to compute vertical scaling. Vertical scaling is commonly used to monitor system-level learning growth on a common proficiency scale as students advance from lower to upper grades.

Source: Original compilation for this publication.

This primer is meant to be an introduction to large-scale assessment topics. Readers interested in these highly technical aspects of large-scale assessments can review the references at the end of this chapter for guidance on sources that cover these topics in detail.

Key Ideas

- All assessment design decisions that the national assessment team makes should support the stated objectives of the assessment and its intended uses.

- Choice of students to be assessed will depend on stakeholder views regarding ages or grade levels that mark key transition points in schooling and at which system-level information on key learning outcomes should be measured.
- The choice between a census- and sample-based approach will depend on assessment objectives and intended uses of assessment results.
- Test content should be aligned with the national curriculum, and this alignment should be codified in the assessment framework.
- Well-written items are straightforward, clear, and designed to provide evidence of specific knowledge, skills, and abilities in line with the assessment framework and test blueprint.
- National large-scale assessments are typically administered in the official language of instruction; however, when the language of instruction differs from the language spoken at home, it may be necessary to make accommodations, particularly for younger students.
- Collecting background information on teachers, classrooms, students, and communities can provide valuable insights into factors that contribute to achievement gaps and suggest pathways for change.
- Countries exploring computer-based test administration should consider the availability of technology in schools and whether computer-based assessments would be fair to all students, given their prior experience with technology.
- The test administration manual should describe the processes and procedures necessary to ensure that every student who participates in the assessment can do so under the same test conditions.
- Design decisions are not permanent and should be revisited as the education system and stakeholder needs change.

References

AERA (American Educational Research Association), APA (American Psychological Association), and NCME (National Council on Measurement in Education). 2014. *Standards for Educational and Psychological Testing.* Washington, DC: AERA.

Agencia de Calidad de la Educación. 2020. "SIMCE." https://www.agenciaeducacion.cl/simce/.

Anderson, Prue, and George Morgan. 2008. *National Assessments of Educational Achievement, Volume 2: Developing Tests and Questionnaires for a National Assessment of Educational Achievement.* Washington, DC: World Bank.

ETS (Educational Testing Service). 2014. *2014 ETS Standards for Quality and Fairness.* Princeton, NJ: ETS.

Greaney, Vincent, and Thomas Kellaghan. 2008. *National Assessments of Educational Achievement, Volume 1: Assessing National Achievement Levels in Education.* Washington, DC: World Bank.

Kafle, Badusev, Shyam Prasad Acharya, and Deviram Acharya. 2019. *National Assessment of Student Achievement 2018. Main Report.* Sanothimi, Bhaktapur: Government of Nepal, Ministry of Education, Science and Technology, Education Review Office.

Ministério da Educação. 2020. "Prova Brasil—Apresentação." http://portal.mec.gov.br/prova-brasil.

NAEP (National Assessment of Education Progress). 2019. "NAEP Assessment Sample Design." https://nces.ed.gov/nationsreportcard/tdw/sample_design/.

Ra, Sungup, Sungsook Kim, and Ki Jong Rhee. 2019. *Developing National Student Assessment Systems for Quality Education: Lessons from the Republic of Korea.* Manila, Philippines: Asian Development Bank.

UNICEF (United Nations Children's Fund) and SEAMEO (Southeast Asian Ministers of Education Organization). 2017. "SEA-PLM 2019 Assessment Framework, 1st Ed." Bangkok, Thailand: UNICEF and SEAMEO. https://www.seaplm.org/PUBLICATIONS/frameworks/sea-plm%202019%20assessment%20framework.pdf.

Wolff, Laurence. 2007. "The Costs of Student Assessments in Latin America." Working Paper No. 38, Partnership for Educational Revitalization in the Americas, Washington, DC.

Chapter 5
WHAT NEEDS TO BE KEPT IN MIND FOR THE IMPLEMENTATION OF LARGE-SCALE ASSESSMENTS?

Activities during the development stage of a large-scale assessment are usually centralized, but the implementation process is decentralized. During the implementation stage, the focus of the national assessment team shifts to navigating the diverse local contexts in which learning takes place.

What Are the Main Considerations for Implementation?

Greaney and Kellaghan (2008, 2012) describe in detail the activities involved in the implementation of a national large-scale assessment. This chapter highlights the most important of those activities that are critical to success during this phase.

COMMUNICATION WITH SCHOOLS

After the school selection process, school administrators should be notified about the participation of their school in the assessment. Schools should be provided with guidelines describing the following:

- Objective of the assessment and how the results will be used
- When the assessment will occur
- Which students will be taking part in the assessment
- How much classroom time will be required to participate
- Space requirements or additional materials that will need to be provided
- How test materials will need to be stored before, during, and after administration.

Schools should also be notified of how they were selected into the sample (if a sample-based approach is being used) and the criteria for selecting classrooms and students to participate. Schools should be assured of the confidentiality of all information collected during the assessment process. Test administrators should actively follow up with schools to confirm their participation a few weeks before the testing date(s); participation should again be confirmed a few days before testing takes place to ensure that materials are available and everyone is prepared for the administration activities.

PACKING MATERIALS

Packing procedures should be established and documented to prevent the loss of booklets and item leakage (Greaney and Kellaghan 2012). Table 5.1 is an example of a packing checklist. This list includes all materials that the national assessment team must provide to participating schools. It should be customized and sufficiently detailed to support assessment delivery and data collection. For example, if students will be completing Scantron answer sheets, HB pencils will need to be provided to ensure that marked answers can be accurately scored. National assessment team members should sign and date the appropriate boxes in the *Packed* and *Returned* columns in the packing checklist. The school liaison should do the same in the boxes in the *Received* column after checking the material sent from the national assessment office. It is recommended that materials be arranged in easy-to-manage units (for example, packages of 20 booklets); additional test booklets and questionnaires be included for unexpected circumstances; and each package be labeled accordingly.

TRANSPORTATION AND STORAGE

The costs, manpower, and resources required to print, securely transport, and store the test materials are often underestimated. Before test administration,

TABLE 5.1. Packing Checklist

Number	Item Date	Packed	Received	Returned
40	Student booklets			
40	Student questionnaires			
45	Pencils			
45	Erasers			
5	Extra booklets			
5	Extra questionnaires			
45	Rubber bands			
3	Self-addressed envelopes			
2	Test administration forms			
1	Student tracking form			

Source: Adapted from Greaney and Kellaghan 2012.

the assessment team should plan for the timely dissemination of the test materials, considering factors such as available delivery methods and the remoteness of some locations. This calculation should also reflect the time required to collect the materials from schools and process test materials.

As noted in chapter 3, secure spaces will be required to store the test materials and organize them before shipment, upon arrival at school sites, and after test administration. During transport, additional packing and resources may be required to ensure that the test materials are not accessed inappropriately or tampered with (Anderson and Morgan 2008). For example, in France, all test materials are packed and sealed in a special black plastic bag that is difficult to open and, once open, cannot be resealed.

MONITORING PARTICIPATION

High levels of participation are important to ensure the reliability and validity of the assessment results. For example, the International Association for the Evaluation of Educational Achievement requires that countries ensure a minimum school participation rate of 85 percent, classroom participation rate of 95 percent, and student participation rate of 85 percent for its Trends in International Mathematics and Science Study (TIMSS) and Progress in International Reading Literacy Study (PIRLS) assessments (Martin, Mullis, and Hooper 2016, 2017). Tracking of participation and nonparticipation of schools, classrooms, and students is critical for management of administrative activities and accurate analysis of data collected from the assessment.

The national large-scale assessment team should maintain a list of schools whose participation is confirmed to help monitor fieldwork progress (table 5.2). In a census-based assessment, schools that do not participate cannot be replaced. In a sample-based assessment, if participation is voluntary, and a school elects not to participate, or there are circumstances that prevent a school's participation, the statistician on the team can identify another school of the same type as a potential replacement. Any school replacements must be appropriately

TABLE 5.2. National Large-Scale Assessment: School Tracking Form

Priority of school[a]	School identification number	Name, address, phone number of school	School size	Status (participant or nonparticipant)	Date materials sent	Date materials received	Date of testing
1							
1							
1							
1							
2							
2							
2							

Source: Adapted from Greaney and Kellaghan 2012.

Note: [a]Schools selected from the sample are priority 1. Replacement schools are priority 2.

selected to maintain sample representativeness, and nonparticipation must be recorded. Greaney and Kellaghan (2012) provide additional information on processes and procedures for school and student replacement.

For participating schools, test administrators must ensure that the classes selected to participate are the ones that actually take part in the assessment, recording any deviations from standard test procedures. In each classroom, administrators must note details pertaining to the participation of individual students: total number of assessed students, whether any students were excluded from taking part in the assessment, students who were absent from school or class, or students who left before completing the assessment.

Figure 5.1 shows a student tracking form. The information recorded on the form usually includes each student's name, assigned identification number, date of birth, gender, and record of attendance at individual testing sessions and, where applicable, replacement sessions. If the testing requires more than one session, the student's presence should be noted for each session.

FIGURE 5.1. National Large-Scale Assessment: Student Tracking Form

School name: ______________________

School ID	Class ID	Class name	Grade

Student Name	Student ID	DOB	Gender	Excluded	Dropout	Session			Replacement Session		

Source: Adapted from Greaney and Kellaghan 2012.
Note: DOB = date of birth.

What Are Some Important Issues to Consider during the Assessment Administration?

TIMING AND TEST SECURITY

Depending on the length of the assessment, it may not be possible for all testing to be completed on the same day, in which case it will be critical for the test administrator to ensure the security of the materials (Greaney and Kellaghan 2008, 2012). The test administrator will need to corroborate that test materials are correctly labeled, collected, and appropriately secured after each testing session. Careful preparation and coordination with schools in advance of the assessment administration can help ensure that adequate space and resources are available to store tests and answer booklets securely.

LOCAL CONDITIONS

Before implementation, test administrators should have received test manuals and attended training sessions to ensure that the test administration procedures are well understood and can be properly executed. Preparation is particularly important, given the wide variation in testing conditions that administrators may encounter, to ensure that students can be seated appropriately and the classroom is free of materials that might distract students or aid their completion of the assessment. It may be helpful to create a checklist for test administrators to review before administration. The following questions are asked by evaluators responsible for quality control of TIMSS (Greaney and Kellaghan 2012).

- Are there adequate numbers of test booklets?
- Are there adequate numbers of student answer sheets?
- Are the test booklets sealed, or have they been tampered with before distribution to students?
- Do classrooms have adequate seating and space for students participating in the assessment?
- Will test administrators in all classrooms have access to a clock, stopwatch, or timer?
- Is there an adequate supply of pencils and other materials?
- If Scantron sheets are being used, is there an adequate supply of HB pencils?

Although test administrators have some control over the classroom environment and testing parameters, they cannot control teacher or student behavior. Students may arrive late to testing sessions or leave before sections of the test are completed. Teachers or school administrators might insist on being present in the classroom during the assessment when their presence is not standard procedure. As with participation, the test administrator should record any deviations from standard procedures (Anderson and Morgan 2008). Figure 5.2 shows a test administration form that could be used in the quality control process and to record any extraordinary events that may occur.

BOOKLET ASSIGNMENT AND IDENTIFICATION

Testing may occur over multiple sessions. Students may record their answers for all sessions in a single test booklet or in multiple booklets (for example, one for each session or subject assessed). Test booklets must be accurately labeled, ensuring that each student's work is appropriately credited. Labels are particularly important when students use multiple booklets, because booklets must be matched for quality control and data analysis after testing has concluded. Test administrators must ensure that students label their booklets consistently, legibly, and with complete information (Greaney and Kellaghan 2012).

FIGURE 5.2. Example of a Test Administration Form

Complete one form per testing session.

Name of test administrator: ______________________

School ID: ______________________

School name: ______________________

Class name: ______________________

School liaison or focal point: ______________________

Original testing session: ______________________

Replacement testing session (if applicable): ______________________

Date of testing: ______________________

Time of testing

Start time	End time	Details
		Administration of test materials
		Testing session 1
		Testing session 2
		Testing session 3
		Testing session 4

1. Did any special circumstances or unusual events occur during the session?

   NO ______

   YES ______ *Please provide the details*

   ____

2. Did students have any particular problems with the testing (*for example, tests too difficult, not enough time provided, language problems, tiring, instructions not clear*)?

   NO ______

   YES ______ *Please provide the details*

   ____

3. Were there any problems with the testing materials (*for example, errors, blank pages, inappropriate language, omissions in the student tracking forms, inadequate numbers of tests or questionnaires*)?

   NO ______

   YES ______ *Please provide the details*

   ____

Source: Adapted from Greaney and Kellaghan 2012.

Key Ideas

- Planning and preparation are critical to successful assessment implementation.
- Regular and early communication with school administrators and school leadership is critical to ensuring the success of a large-scale assessment exercise. School administrators must understand who will be assessed, why the assessment is taking place in their school, what will be assessed, and how long the assessment will take so that they can plan accordingly.
- Tracking school and student participation and nonparticipation is important for the management of assessment administration and analysis of resulting data.
- Checklists and standard forms can help track the assembly, use, dissemination, and return of test materials.
- Resource costs and time required for organizing, securely packaging, and transporting test materials must be accounted for and are often underestimated in budget plans.
- Checklists and forms can help ensure that test administrators are prepared for conducting the assessment according to the procedures described in the test administration manual.
- Monitoring and reporting local conditions at the time of the assessment is important for accountability and continuous improvement of assessment activities.

References

Anderson, Prue, and George Morgan. 2008. *National Assessments of Educational Achievement, Volume 2: Developing Tests and Questionnaires for a National Assessment of Educational Achievement*. Washington, DC: World Bank.

Greaney, Vincent, and Thomas Kellaghan. 2008. *National Assessments of Educational Achievement, Volume 1: Assessing National Achievement Levels in Education*. Washington, DC: World Bank.

Greaney, Vincent, and Thomas Kellaghan. 2012. *National Assessments of Educational Achievement, Volume 3: Implementing a National Assessment of Educational Achievement*. Washington, DC: World Bank.

Martin, Michael O., Ina V. S. Mullis, and Martin Hooper, eds. 2016. *Methods and Procedures in TIMSS 2015*. Boston, MA: TIMSS and PIRLS International Study Center. http://timssandpirls.bc.edu/publications/timss/2015-methods.html.

Martin, Michael O., Ina V. S. Mullis, and Martin Hooper, eds. 2017. *Methods and Procedures in PIRLS 2016*. Boston, MA: TIMSS and PIRLS International Study Center. https://timssandpirls.bc.edu/publications/pirls/2016-methods.html.

Chapter 6 WHAT ARE THE CRITICAL STEPS IN THE ANALYSIS OF LARGE-SCALE ASSESSMENT DATA?

After the test is administered, the national assessment team must make sense of the data. The purpose of this chapter is to provide an overview of the main analytic activities that should be conducted after test administration: scoring and summarizing student performance, coding data from background questionnaires, and conducting basic analyses to summarize findings that will be included in the main report on the assessment exercise.

Assessment reports typically include descriptive analyses that summarize overall student performance and average performance of relevant subgroups, such as male versus female students and those in public versus private schools. Assessment reports may also include in-depth analyses exploring the relationships between contextual factors and student achievement. Findings are presented narratively and supported with tables and charts to facilitate understanding by a broad stakeholder audience (Shiel and Cartwright 2015).

How Are Tests and Questionnaires Scored and Coded?

After the test administration, the student responses must be scored and recorded for analysis. National assessment teams must allocate enough time, space, and resources to accomplish these data management tasks. Adequately resourcing data management tasks is critical because having accurate data is a prerequisite for statistical analyses to be conducted (Shiel and Cartwright 2015).

Data management involves the documentation, organization, and storage of collected data. Good data management practices help ensure consistency in how information is collected, coded, and arranged for data analysis. Data management procedures also reduce the chance of errors that could go undetected throughout the life of a project. Particularly as the volume of data increases, assessment teams will benefit from having a clear plan and protocols for data management, as well as staff with relevant expertise, including statisticians and information technology specialists.

Assessment teams should develop a data codebook that describes each variable in the data file and defines the values permitted for each. The codebook maps each item in the assessment to its variable label in the data set, variable codes for the response options, variable formats, and codes for missing values (Shiel and Cartwright 2015).

Enumerators responsible for scoring multiple-choice items will need an answer key with the correct response options identified for each item. The codebook identifies for enumerators which codes are to be entered into the database for a correct response, incorrect response, missing information when no answer is provided, or instances when a student inappropriately selects multiple options (box 6.1).

Most codebooks are developed using Microsoft Excel and Microsoft Word because these files can be easily saved and exported to other file formats. Codebooks communicate to external specialists the meaning of each variable and its associated values, thereby supporting their ability to conduct data analysis without continuous guidance from the team responsible for data collection and coding.

BOX 6.1. Example of an Item and Its Codebook Information

Item 6. Reading comprehension

6. According to the text, Sara and her family went to the __________

A. river

B. beach *

C. country

D. mountains

Item: 6. According to the text, Sara and her family went to the __________

Variable name: item 6

Correct response: B.

Codes for response options.

(1) Correct answer.

(0) Incorrect answer.

(−999) Missing value.

Note: Any other value is considered invalid.

Source: Original compilation for this publication.

Open-ended and short-response items require written rubrics to evaluate student responses, which should be included in the codebook (box 6.2). Enumerators should have clear scoring rules accompanied by examples showing how illegible or unclear responses must be scored. Anderson and Morgan (2008)

BOX 6.2. Scoring Rubrics

A scoring rubric is a set of scoring guidelines with examples or descriptors of the potential range of student responses that facilitates the reliable scoring of open-ended responses. It is essential for the assessment team to confirm that the scoring guidelines are appropriate for all planned analyses.

An example of a scoring rubric from the regional large-scale assessment for Latin America, Laboratorio Latinoamericano de Evaluación de la Calidad de la Educación (LLECE), is shown below. LLECE is reviewed in detail in chapter 9. The LLECE language assessment administered in 2013 includes a writing task that is scored using a rubric with eight indicators. Each indicator has four levels of performance. The indicator *Genre* is shown below. The task for the student is to write a letter to a friend; this indicator scores whether the authored letter contains all of the formal elements it would be expected to include. As shown, scoring guidelines should describe the characteristics of student responses across the full range of student proficiency to help raters score answers reliably. In addition, the guidelines should be written to ensure a high degree of interrater reliability, which means that multiple raters who read the same response to an open-ended item would score it similarly.

Pilot studies offer valuable opportunities to gather evidence on any revisions that should be made to scoring rubrics. The range of student responses received during a pilot can inform revision of these scoring guides and associated examples to ensure that they reflect actual rather than idealized ranges of student performance.

Writing rubric indicator and dimensions in LLECE 2013

Indicator 1b. Genre. This indicator measures the ability to act based on a socially established text model considered appropriate to solving a communication problem. In this case, genre is understood as the prototypical, relatively stable, socially acceptable way in which texts are used in society. The purpose is not only to assess the formal aspects of text genres in terms of knowledge, but also to characterize the use of discourse markers for a given communicative purpose (for example, presence of greeting, orientation to a recipient).

Proficiency levels and descriptors

Level 1. The written text is not a letter, but something that belongs to a different genre (for example, dialogue or short story).

Level 2. The written text is a letter including only the body of the letter but without a clear message targeted to the recipient.

Level 3. The written text includes the body of the letter in addition to a greeting at the beginning or a goodbye message to the recipient at the end.

Level 4. The written text includes a formal greeting at the beginning, the body of the letter, and a goodbye message to the recipient at the end.

Source: Adapted from Flotts et al. 2016.

describe in detail how teams of enumerators should be structured to ensure that student responses to open-ended items are accurately scored. Greaney and Kellaghan (2008, 2012) describe in detail additional steps in the data management and data entry processes.

What Are Sampling Weights?

Before any analysis, including calculation of descriptive summaries of student achievement, the assessment records must be organized and matched with any demographic or questionnaire data. In the case of sample-based assessments that employ complex survey designs for data collection, sampling weights must be calculated and applied to student responses (Shiel and Cartwright 2015). Application of sampling weights ensures that the information derived from the sample is an accurate representation of the broader student population. Readers interested in this topic are encouraged to review Shiel and Cartwright (2015), which addresses sampling weights and how to perform a variety of descriptive and inferential statistical analyses that incorporate sampling weights.

What Are Common Ways to Describe Student Achievement?

Providing a summary of student performance, overall and for particular subgroups, is the core of the main assessment report. Numerical summaries should describe the performance of the typical or average student and provide readers with information about variability in student achievement. The following section provides a brief conceptual overview of some of the ways that assessment teams may summarize and communicate results from an assessment to key stakeholders (Shiel and Cartwright 2015).

PERCENTAGE CORRECT

One way to capture student performance is to report the percentage of items answered correctly, which can also be compared across different subgroups. Table 6.1 presents the percentage-correct results for Ghana's national assessments of English and mathematics, according to sex. It shows that the percentage of correctly answered mathematics items in grade 4 is similar for boys and girls; however, boys answered more items correctly on the grade 6 mathematics assessment, girls had a higher percentage of correctly answered items on the grade 4 English assessment, and boys and girls performed similarly on the grade 6 English assessment.

Reporting test results in this way is a useful starting point for understanding how students performed on the test, but it does not answer many questions that are likely to be important to stakeholders: What was the range of variation in performance on the test? Are students from certain groups more likely to perform better or worse than others? Moreover, stakeholders may be interested in knowing how many students demonstrated mastery of the content being examined. Answering these questions requires that assessment teams describe the variation in student achievement and characterize student performance relative to norms or standards (Shiel and Cartwright 2015).

TABLE 6.1. Percentage of Correct Answers on Ghana's National Large-Scale Assessment According to Sex

Assessment	Male (percent)	Female (percent)
Mathematics grade 4	41.9	41.5
Mathematics grade 6	44.9	42.8
English grade 4	49.8	52.0
English grade 6	47.6	48.1

Source: Ministry of Education, Ghana Education Service, and National Education Assessment Unit 2016.

Note: Results are presented as percentage of items correctly answered in each assessment.

NORM-REFERENCED ASSESSMENT REPORTING

Norm-referenced reporting involves describing student performance in terms of the characteristics of the statistical distribution of student test scores. The results for each student are compared with the average or typical proficiency of all tested students. Typical student performance might be captured using the mean or arithmetic average, the median or midpoint of the score distribution, or the mode or most commonly achieved score. Most national large-scale assessments use the mean or arithmetic average. In addition to average levels of achievement, score reporting should include information about variation in student test scores, such as the possible and observed upper and lower range of scores. Including measures of variability in student performance provides stakeholders with a more complete picture of student achievement and prevents overinterpretation of differences in average performance (Shiel and Cartwright 2015).

Figure 6.1 summarizes the results for the language and communication and mathematics sections of Chile's national large-scale assessment. The two bars on the left side of the graph represent the overall national average in these two subjects. Regional average scores are represented in the subsequent bars, with the number at the top of each bar being the region's average score. The regional scores in red are significantly different from the national average scores.

Norm-referenced reporting of test results can support the comparison of subgroups in a sample of student performance over time, although this form of reporting does not map directly to test content. If stakeholders are interested in understanding the students' level of mastery of a domain or which skills they have acquired, they can better do so using a standards-referenced approach.

STANDARDS-REFERENCED REPORTING

National large-scale assessments are increasingly using a *standards-referenced* approach to report results. Standards-referenced reporting involves describing student performance in terms of what they know and can do in relation to domain-specific achievement standards. Instead of numeric scores, results are reported using descriptions of the tasks that students are able to perform, such as reading "at a basic level of comprehension" or performing "advanced mathematical operations." Defining and setting standards is a complex task that requires the involvement of curriculum experts and statistical analysts; readers interested in exploring the topic of standard-setting in detail are encouraged to consult Shiel and Cartwright (2015).

Figure 6.2 shows the percentage of students falling into different performance levels on Peru's national large-scale assessment of reading. The results are broken out according to rural versus urban status in 2016 and 2018. Students in urban areas were more likely to reach the highest performance level on the assessment in both years.

FIGURE 6.1. Results of Chile's National Large-Scale Assessment, According to State

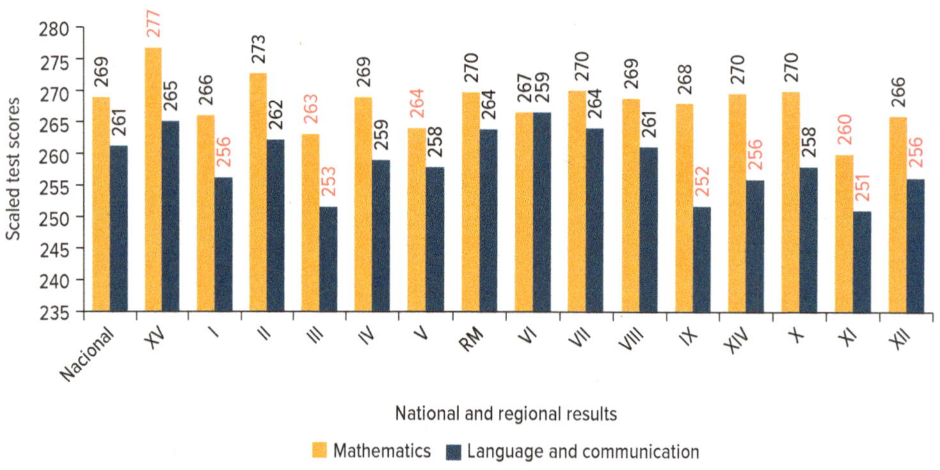

Source: Adapted from Agencia de Calidad de la Educación 2019.

Note: RM = Region Metropolitana of the City of Santiago.

FIGURE 6.2. Peru's National Large-Scale Assessment Results, According to Rural versus Urban Location, 2016 and 2018

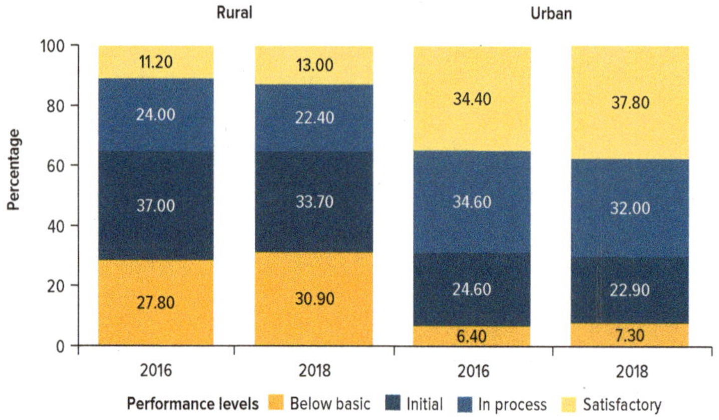

Source: Adapted from Ministerio de Educación 2019.

What Are Some Basic Analyses to Determine Which Factors Affect Student Achievement?

Various analyses can be performed to determine which factors affect student achievement.

EXPLORING RELATIONSHIPS USING CORRELATIONS

A national large-scale assessment should inform discussions about how to improve learning outcomes. Analyses that find relationships between student achievement and specific factors covered in the background questionnaires can be particularly useful in this regard. For example, policy makers and other stakeholders may be interested in knowing whether there is a relationship between student attendance at school and mathematics achievement, or between time spent doing homework and literacy skills. Different relationships might suggest different policies to improve learning outcomes (Shiel and Cartwright 2015).

Correlations are a common way to characterize the direction and strength of the relationship between test scores and other variables. For example, if we observe a strong positive correlation between school attendance and math scores, we may conclude that the more students attend school, the more likely they are to have better mathematics performance. In parallel, if we observe a negative correlation between school absenteeism and mathematics achievement, we may assume that the more days of absence from school, the more likely a student is to demonstrate poor performance in math. However, such correlations do not guarantee causation. For example, a high negative correlation between absenteeism and math scores does not necessarily mean that absenteeism *causes* students to have lower mathematics proficiency. The distinction between correlation and causation is discussed more in the next section.

Correlations can also be used to understand relationships between student performance on different assessments of the same domain, competency, or skill. Table 6.2 shows correlations between Swedish students' mathematics proficiency, as measured on the Trends in International Mathematics and Science Study (TIMSS) grade 8 assessment, and four alternative measures of mathematics performance: student mathematics proficiency scores on grades 6 and 9 national large-scale assessments and grades earned upon completing the grades 6 and 9 math curricula (Wiberg 2019). All correlation coefficients are positive, indicating that children demonstrating higher achievement on the TIMSS mathematics assessment also tend to perform well in school and are likely to earn higher scores on Sweden's national tests. This is an expected result, given that there is a high degree of alignment, particularly between the grade 9 mathematics curriculum and what the TIMSS assessment measures. Results like these would be particularly relevant to a national assessment team interested in providing evidence of the validity of the national large-scale assessment in terms of being able to measure student performance in core areas of mathematics.

TABLE 6.2. Correlation between Grade 8 Trends in International Mathematics and Science Study Mathematics Achievement and School Measures of Mathematics Achievement, According to Sex: Sweden

	Grade 6		Grade 9	
	Mathematics grade	National large-scale assessment	Mathematics grade	National large-scale assessment
Boys	0.69	0.67	0.74	0.66
Girls	0.69	0.68	0.74	0.66

Source: Adapted from Wiberg 2019.

CORRELATION VERSUS CAUSATION

Although correlation coefficients can be useful, it is important that they not be misinterpreted as evidence of causal relationships. Establishing causation requires a specific relationship between contextual variables (for example, attendance) and outcome variables (for example, mathematics achievement) characterized by covariation, temporal precedence, and nonspuriousness.

- *Covariation.* This means that as the contextual variable increases or decreases in value, the corresponding value of the outcome variable also tends to increase or decrease.
- *Temporal precedence.* For a contextual variable to cause an outcome, that contextual variable must measure an action, characteristic, or behavior that occurs *before* the outcome.
- *Nonspuriousness.* There cannot be a different variable or set of variables that explains the observed association between the contextual variable and the outcome variable. In an experiment, this is guaranteed by comparing outcomes from a control group that was not exposed to the treatment variable with outcomes from a group that was exposed.

Causation is difficult to establish using data from large-scale assessments because they typically have a cross-sectional design, meaning that contextual information and data on student performance are captured at the same time. Therefore, it not possible to establish temporal precedence using large-scale assessment data.

Causation is also difficult to establish using assessment data because assessments are not experiments, and there is no control group. Therefore, it is not possible to isolate the effect of one or even a set of contextual factors on educational outcomes. A wide range of factors is associated with student learning achievement; many of them are interrelated, including features of the classroom environment and instructional practices, as well as characteristics of students, their families, and the communities in which they live. It is not feasible to capture information on all of these factors during a national assessment, given the practical constraints of time and budget and the potential sensitivities of data collection. Falsely asserting that there is a causal relationship when one has not been established can lead to ineffective or even counterproductive policies.

What Are Test Score Validity and Reliability?

Evidence of test score validity and reliability must be documented in the main findings report or in the assessment technical report. Reporting this information can help stakeholders determine the accuracy of the assessment results, correctly interpret results, and use them as intended.

VALIDITY

Validity requires continuous accumulation of evidence to support or dispute the interpretation of test scores, the use of test results, and the intended consequences of their use (Martone and Sireci 2009; Sireci 2009). There are five general sources of evidence in the current validity framework (AERA, APA, and NCME 2014). Table 6.3 summarizes the five sources of validity evidence and provides examples of the types of studies used to document each of them. Depending on the assessment objectives and intended uses of scores, more effort is put into gathering and documenting some sources of evidence than others.

RELIABILITY

In addition to validity, it is essential that test scores characterize student achievement reliably and accurately. Reliability is related to the internal consistency of items, the score equivalence between test forms, and the score stability over time, which reduces the potential sources of measurement error. For open-response items, reliability also should be established across test enumerators or raters who score student responses. According to current standards of psychological and educational testing, assessments are expected to have high score reliability when there are consequences for examinees and other stakeholders based on the results (AERA, APA, and NCME 2014). Table 6.4 lists the potential sources of measurement error and the psychometric coefficients commonly reported to describe the reliability properties of an

TABLE 6.3. Five Sources of Validity Evidence and Examples

Source of validity evidence	Examples of potential empirical studies to document validity evidence
Test content	• Subject matter expert review of items and their alignment with the national curriculum
Cognitive processes	• Think-aloud interviews of examinees (examinees thinking aloud as they are responding to items on the test) • Examinee feedback • Use of anchor examples of expected student responses in rubrics
Internal structure	• Inter-item correlations using exploratory and confirmatory factor analysis
Association between test scores and external variables	• Correlation between test scores and external variables
Consequences of the use of the test	• Alignment of assessment objectives and use • Analysis of intended consequences linked to use of assessment

Source: Sireci 2009.

TABLE 6.4. Sources of Bias and Reliability

Source of bias or error	Reliability coefficient	Data collection procedure	Statistical analysis
Content covered in a single test form with potentially biased items	Internal consistency coefficient	Administration of one test form on a single occasion	Cronbach's alpha coefficient
Short-term changes in an examinee's performance due to nontest factors	Temporal stability coefficient	Administer the test, wait, retest with the same test form	Pearson correlation coefficient
Differences in content covered by two test forms measuring the same construct	Equivalence coefficient	Administration of forms A and B to the same examinees	Pearson correlation coefficient
Rater scoring bias	Interrater agreement coefficient	Two raters scoring the same stimulus using the same rubric or scoring tool	Cohen's kappa coefficient

Source: Authors' compilation for this publication.

assessment tool. Depending on the intended uses of the results, one or more studies will be implemented to quantify score reliability and the amount of measurement error.

Should Assessment Data, Codebooks, and Technical Reports Be Made Publicly Available?

Most assessment agencies will be limited in terms of the human resources and the time available to explore all possible relationships between the many factors that may influence student achievement, particularly when the time between the dissemination of assessment results and the planning for the next large-scale assessment is limited. In many countries, national large-scale assessment data and all supporting materials are made publicly available for external stakeholders (for example, researchers at universities, civil society organizations, and international development organizations) interested in conducting secondary data analysis. The national assessment team must ensure that data do not contain personally identifiable student information before making them public.

Making data and supporting materials—such as codebooks, technical reports, and statistical code—publicly available can have several benefits:

- It allows external experts to perform additional analyses, which can complement and expand on findings from the national assessment agency.
- It makes the national assessment agency's work more relevant, particularly when external stakeholders understand the value of the assessment data.
- It promotes innovation in the work of assessment agencies by allowing external stakeholders to explore existing data and identify original findings that can motivate policy dialogue and new initiatives.
- It encourages collaboration between the national assessment agency and external stakeholders and more external stakeholder participation in future assessment initiatives.

Key Ideas

- After test administration, national assessment teams must allocate time, space, and resources to score and record student responses. Advance planning for these activities becomes more important as the volume of data being collected increases.
- When student responses are scored and recorded, it is important that assessment teams develop a data codebook that maps each assessment item to its variable label in the data set, variable codes for the response options, variable formats, and codes for missing values.
- Codebooks are valuable resources internally for the team and externally for stakeholders to conduct secondary analyses.
- Providing a summary description of student performance constitutes the core of the main results report. The approach used to summarize and report on student performance should be determined during test development and driven by the information needs of stakeholders.
- Norm-referenced reporting answers questions about the average proficiency of students who completed the assessment and the types of students who are more likely to perform above or below average.
- Standard-referenced reporting is increasingly common and addresses questions about what students know and can do and which students have mastered the expected learning content.
- Correlation coefficients are commonly used to describe the relationship between contextual factors and student achievement.
- Correlation is not causation, and causal relationships are difficult to establish using data typically collected from large-scale assessments.

References

AERA (American Educational Research Association), APA (American Psychological Association), and NCME (National Council on Measurement in Education). 2014. *Standards for Educational and Psychological Testing*. Washington, DC: AERA.

Agencia de Calidad de la Educación. 2019. "Informe Nacional de la Calidad de la Educación 2018." http://archivos.agenciaeducacion.cl/libro_informe_nacional.pdf.

Anderson, Prue, and George Morgan. 2008. *National Assessments of Educational Achievement, Volume 2: Developing Tests and Questionnaires for a National Assessment of Educational Achievement*. Washington, DC: World Bank.

Flotts, Paulina, Jorge Manzi, Daniela Jimenez, Andrea Abarzua, Carlos Cayuman, and Maria José Garcia. 2016. *Informe de Resultados. Tercer Estudio Regional Comparativo y Explicativo*. Santiago, Chile: UNESCO.

Greaney, Vincent, and Thomas Kellaghan. 2008. *National Assessments of Educational Achievement, Volume 1: Assessing National Achievement Levels in Education*. Washington, DC: World Bank.

Greaney, Vincent, and Thomas Kellaghan. 2012. *National Assessments of Educational Achievement, Volume 3: Implementing a National Assessment of Educational Achievement*. Washington, DC: World Bank.

Martone, Andrea, and Stephen G. Sireci. 2009. "Evaluating Alignment Between Curriculum, Assessment, and Instruction." *Review of Educational Research* 79 (4): 1332–61.

Ministerio de Educación. 2019. "Oficina de Medición de la Calidad de los Aprendizajes: Evaluación." http://umc.minedu.gob.pe/ece2018/#1553619963598-f0a822b6-7323.

Ministry of Education, Ghana Education Service, and National Education Assessment Unit. 2016. "Ghana 2016 Education Assessment. Report of Findings." https://sapghana.com/data/documents/2016-NEA-Findings-Report_17Nov2016_Public-FINAL.pdf.

Shiel, Gerry, and Fernando Cartwright. 2015. *National Assessments of Educational Achievement, Volume 4. Analyzing Data from a National Assessment of Educational Achievement*. Washington, DC: World Bank.

Sireci, Stephen G. 2009. "Packing and Unpacking Sources of Validity Evidence: History Repeats Itself Again." In *The Concept of Validity: Revisions, New Directions and Applications,* edited by R. Lissitz, 19–39. Charlotte, NC: Information Age.

Wiberg, Marie. 2019. "The Relationship Between TIMSS Mathematics Achievements, Grades, and National Test Scores." *Education Inquiry* 10 (4): 328–43.

Chapter 7
HOW CAN EFFECTIVE COMMUNICATION OF LARGE-SCALE ASSESSMENT RESULTS BE ENSURED?

For the results of a national large-scale assessment to affect policy decisions and educational practices, results must be clearly and consistently communicated. Instead of a single report, multiple communication products may need to be produced to meet the needs of a broad range of stakeholders: policy makers, teachers, school administrators, textbook authors, teacher trainers, curriculum development professionals, parents, and students. The national large-scale assessment results also need to be communicated effectively to the general public to raise awareness of the current state of educational practices and influence public opinion regarding proposed changes to educational policy (Greaney and Kellaghan 2008).

The diversity of interests and wide variation in technical ability among stakeholder groups can present a challenge to national assessment teams responsible for disseminating results. Although assessment teams in some countries issue a single report after administration of a national large-scale assessment, some countries have the capacity to generate multiple reports and information products tailored to specific groups of stakeholders.

Because stakeholders' information needs and interests are so diverse, national assessment teams commonly develop a plan for reporting key findings to different stakeholders. The assessment team must ensure that stakeholders are provided with information that is clear, complete, and targeted to the intended audience. Although every stakeholder group could benefit from a separate report or presentation of results, the assessment team must work within the constraints of time and budget. The team must prioritize development and dissemination of products that will most significantly affect policy and practice, because it will always be possible to generate more informational products than available resources can support.

This chapter gives a brief overview of general principles and guidelines for developing and disseminating reports on national large-scale assessment findings. A detailed discussion can be found in Kellaghan, Greaney, and Murray (2009).

What Are Some Key Guidelines for Reporting Results?

Regardless of how the national assessment team decides to communicate assessment findings—in a series of memos, technical and thematic reports, presentations, or through other information dissemination channels—some general principles should guide the production of those materials.

First, all reports should be factual. Any reported findings should be based on analyses that are well reasoned, defensible, and statistically sound. Academic literature or prior research studies can help contextualize findings, but reports should focus on the results of the assessment. Key takeaways for the targeted audience of the report should be clearly stated in nontechnical language. Where appropriate, narrative descriptions should be reinforced with charts, graphics, or tables that highlight differences in student performance within and between subgroups. Results must be presented in a way that indicates whether observed differences between subgroups or changes over time are statistically significant.

Information products should highlight assessment objectives; emphasize appropriate use of assessment results; and to the extent possible, prevent misinterpretation of results. Descriptions of student performance should showcase the strengths and weaknesses of the national curriculum and education system. Results should be connected to policies or practices in critical areas, such as curriculum development, textbook development, and teacher training. Equally important, reports should acknowledge factors that influence student performance that are outside of the education system and not within teachers' control (Kellaghan, Greaney, and Murray 2009).

What Should Be Covered in the Main Report of Large-Scale Assessment Results?

In some countries, national assessment teams issue a single report after a national large-scale assessment is administered; this single report describes the purpose and context of the assessment, its framework and relationship with the national curriculum and national learning goals, and its methodology. This report should be timely (issued within one year of the assessment administration) and emphasize high-level results. The report should describe overall student performance on the assessment, differences in performance between relevant student subgroups (for example, between boys and girls or between urban and rural students) and, where applicable, changes in performance levels from the last time the assessment was administered. The report could also include information regarding contextual factors that impact student achievement. The report should balance accessibility to a nontechnical audience with the need to provide sufficiently detailed information about the assessment objectives, how the assessment was conducted, its key findings, and policy implications.

OBJECTIVES

The main objectives of the national large-scale assessment should be clearly stated in simple language for a broad audience. Readers of the report should be informed about the questions the assessment is intended to answer, as well as the policy goals and objectives the assessment was designed to inform. Box 7.1 lists some of the main features of education systems about which a national assessment can provide useful information (Kellaghan, Greaney, and Murray 2009).

METHODS

How the national large-scale assessment was designed to answer policy makers' questions and meet the study objectives should be clearly stated. This section may describe the standards and procedures followed to ensure the quality of the assessment tools and the data collection process. Readers should also know the

BOX 7.1. Features That a National Large-Scale Assessment Can Highlight

Access. Obstacles to attending school, such as limited availability of places or distance of students' homes from school.

Quality. Quality of inputs to and outputs of schooling, such as resources and facilities available to support learning (responsive curricula, teacher competence, textbooks), instructional practices, student-teacher interactions, and student learning.

Efficiency. Optimal use of human and financial resources, reflected in student-teacher ratios, number of students enrolled in the education system, and grade repetition rates.

Equity. Provision of educational opportunities to students and attainment of parity of achievement for students, irrespective of their characteristics, such as gender, language or ethnic group membership, and geographic location.

Source: Kellaghan, Greaney, and Murray 2009.

characteristics of the students who participated in the assessment and how they were identified and selected, including any sampling procedures used to select schools and students. This information will help readers judge the overall technical quality of the assessment instruments and results.

FINDINGS

The body of the report should provide a robust description of findings linked to student achievement. This section should detail what students know, understand, and can do in each of the domains or curricular areas that the assessment addressed. Student performance is often described in terms of mastery or proficiency levels within each domain, measuring actual student achievement against national learning objectives and target outcomes.

In addition to providing an aggregated summary of student achievement, the main report should explore the performance of different subgroups. The main report should address the question of how well the educational system is performing overall and whether it is serving all students equally well. For instance, depending on the purpose and design of the assessment, the report may contrast performance of urban and rural locations, different geographic regions, or different school types; results may be presented according to gender, ethnic background, or language spoken at home. The report may also include in-depth analyses of the students classified in the lower proficiency levels, what they know and can do, and where they need additional support. When appropriate, the report may explore overall trends in student achievement over time (Kellaghan, Greaney, and Murray 2009).

Discussions about factors linked to student achievement are likely to be sensitive and prone to misinterpretation by some stakeholders. When presenting these findings, the main report should augment narrative descriptions with charts, tables, and graphics. India's 2015 and 2017 National Achievement Survey reports use a variety of visuals to highlight key findings (NCERT 2015, 2017). The graphics provide clear, concise summaries of differences in performance between groups of students (figure 7.1) and between groups of low- and high-performing states (figure 7.2). Tables display results in a compact format that makes it easy for readers to make comparisons (figure 7.3).

POLICY IMPLICATIONS

While remaining factual, the report should discuss the main implications of the findings for the policy questions that motivated the assessment and the extent to which the results are evidence of the need for action. Assessment reports can contribute to a national dialogue on reforms and programs that could improve student learning outcomes and the education system as a whole. As discussed in chapter 2, findings may suggest how a country's resources should be invested to have the greatest effect. Results from an assessment may identify a gap between the design of the national curriculum and its classroom implementation, as well as opportunities for

FIGURE 7.1. Comparison of Student Subgroups from India's 2015 National Achievement Survey

An encouraging finding was reported on the gender-wise parameter, where it was found that on an average, girls are doing better than boys in all subjects.

No significant difference was found in the performance of students from rural or urban backgrounds.

Performance of SC/ST students was significantly below the "Others" category of students.

Performance of students on an average, in Cycle 4 as compared to Cycle 3, had gone down.

Source: Adapted from NCERT 2015.

Note: SC = Scheduled Caste; ST = Scheduled Tribe.

modification of classroom practices. Reports can also inform pre-service and in-service teacher training opportunities, the content of instructional materials for teachers, and curriculum development (Kellaghan, Greaney, and Murray 2009).

Box 7.2 summarizes some of the uses and policy implications of the national large-scale assessment results in the Republic of Korea. Korea's national large-scale assessment has been used to determine school quality and school accountability; at the same time, the assessment results have supported implementation of tailored programs for students and system-level policies for schools.

FIGURE 7.2. Comparison of Response Profiles for Low- and High-Performing States on India's 2017 National Achievement Survey

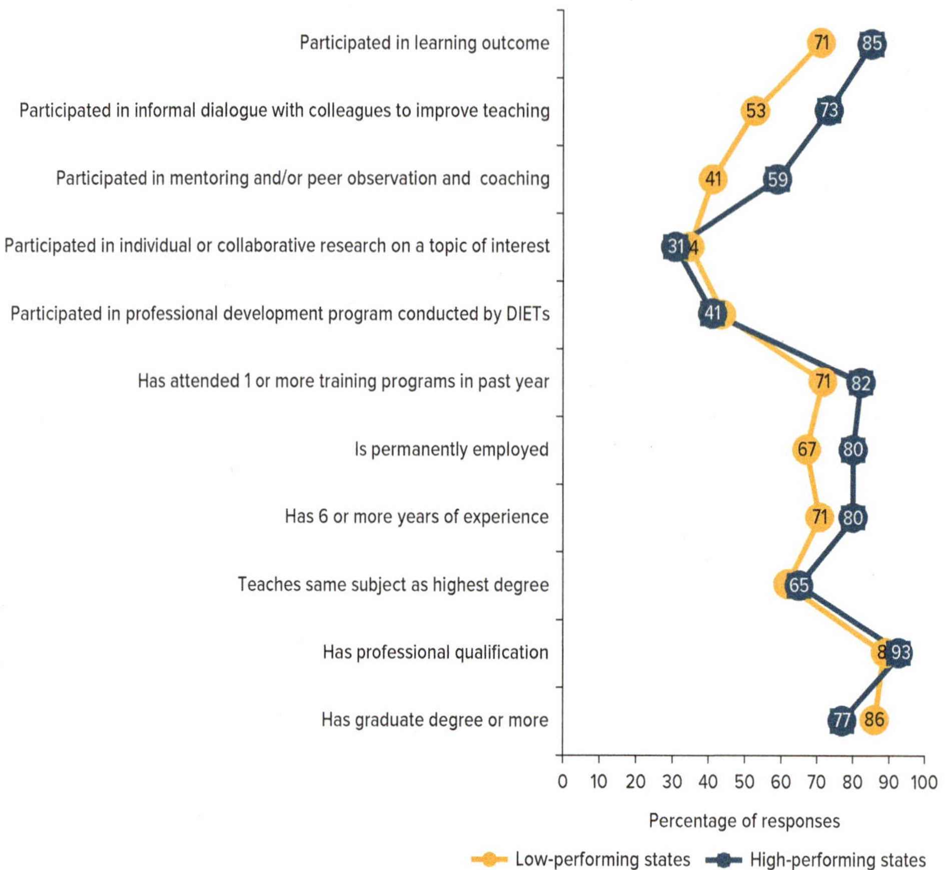

Source: Adapted from NCERT 2017.

Note: DIET = District Institute of Education and Training.

FIGURE 7.3. Comparison of Class V Mean Student Performance in Language, According to State, from India's 2017 National Achievement Survey

State/Union Territories	Mean	State/Union Territories	Mean	State/Union Territories	Mean
Kerala	353	Manipur	320	Punjab	306
Karnataka	351	**National Mean**	**319**	Lakshadweep	304
Chandigarh	345	West Bengal	317	Odisha	304
Rajasthan	344	Tripura	316	Delhi	303
Andhra Pradesh	339	Bihar	316	Mizoram	301
Uttarakhand	338	Telangana	314	Daman and Diu	300
Dadra and Nagar Haveli	335	Madhya Pradesh	313	Puducherry	300
Himachal Pradesh	328	Goa	313	Uttar Pradesh	300
Jharkhand	326	Chhattisgarh	313	Sikkim	297
Gujarat	324	Nagaland	312	Meghalaya	296

■ Significantly above the national average
■ Not significantly different from national average
■ Significantly below the national average

Source: Adapted from NCERT 2017.

BOX 7.2. Policy Implications of National Large-Scale Assessment Results in the Republic of Korea

- *More publicly available information on school quality.* Indices of school performance and progress are developed to explain year-to-year improvement in academic achievement at the school level.
- *Greater school accountability and expanded educational choices.* Public disclosure of assessment results motivates change in educational policy and informs educational choices of students and parents.
- *Greater support of low-achieving students.* The Zero Plan policy initiative identifies schools with a high proportion of students who score below the minimum proficiency level. The Ministry of Education provides administrative and financial support to these schools to improve academic achievement. Tailored programs addressing individual student needs have been implemented to provide targeted support, including learning coaching and psychological counseling.
- *Systemwide policy changes.* Results from the national assessment have been used to implement systemwide policies and comprehensive strategies focused on school leadership, staffing, school climate, instructional practice, and community support.

Source: Ra, Kim, and Rhee 2019.

What Are Other Ways to Communicate Large-Scale Assessment Results?

In addition to the main report, many national assessment teams issue a technical report that describes the assessment framework, test development process, sampling methodology, scoring, and data analysis in detail. The technical report helps specialists evaluate the technical properties of the assessment critically, increases transparency in the assessment process, and informs and improves future assessment practice (Kellaghan, Greaney, and Murray 2009).

The assessment team may also elect to issue one or more thematic reports to provide in-depth analyses of specific questions and seek to present the results of those analyses in a way that is accessible to a broad audience. These thematic reports can also highlight the main takeaways for policy makers. For instance, some countries may develop thematic reports on girls' education, education in the early grades, or skills for the labor force.

Reports are generally expensive to produce, publish, and distribute. These costs may be an additional financial burden in many developing countries; with the availability of technology and internet access, publishing materials online can help mitigate these costs, but it may reduce access to the results by some stakeholder groups with limited infrastructure and technology availability.

Box 7.3 summarizes how the government of Peru has used online technologies to disseminate the results of its national large-scale assessment. The official website of the Peruvian Ministry of Education compiles electronic versions of all assessment reports, as well as press releases; photographs; and audio and video material related to the assessment process, findings, and uses.

Reports are one of many ways that national assessment teams can communicate results to a broad audience effectively. Television, radio, internet, and other forms of media are also valuable ways to communicate results to a wide array of stakeholders. For instance, Ghana's National Council for Curriculum and Assessment uses social media platforms (for example, Facebook, YouTube, and LinkedIn) to disseminate information on its national large-scale assessment results. The national assessment team may also wish to issue a press brief and hold a press conference.

The assessment team may develop information products that are tailored to particular stakeholder groups and that highlight key policy implications of the assessment findings for that group, for instance, concise policy memorandums to personnel in the Ministry of Education on lack of equity highlighted in the results. Assessment results also can be used to inform presentations or workshops at professional conferences or training seminars for teachers and curriculum development professionals. Assessment teams are increasingly making anonymized microdata available so that members of the scientific community can conduct additional analyses to assist in policy and decision-making.

The assessment team should agree on the core set of findings and messages that will be communicated in all formats and should anticipate questions and develop standard answers that reinforce those messages and possibly address misconceptions or misinterpretations. Kellaghan, Greaney, and Murray (2009) discuss the components of a comprehensive media strategy in detail.

BOX 7.3. Online Dissemination of National Large-Scale Assessment Findings in Peru

Peru's Ministry of Education uses digital platforms to disseminate assessment results. Assessment reports are organized according to topic:

- *National assessment reports*: Compilation of main reports, organized according to year of administration and school grade
- *Pedagogical reports*: Archive of reports on assessment results, according to subject and school grade, with a focus on educational recommendations for schools and teachers
- *Methodological and technical reports*: Technical reports focused on statistical and psychometric properties of national assessment tools
- *Brief studies*: Short publications focused on exploring the effect of specific factors on student achievement or lessons learned during project implementation
- *In-depth studies*: Detailed studies on the effect of specific factors on student achievement, such as the influence of school infrastructure on student learning and the relationship between school leadership and student achievement.

An additional online section includes press releases from the assessment agency. This information is cataloged as follows:

- *Assessment news*: News related to the release and use of national large-scale assessment results for improvement of the education system
- *Audio material*: Audio files targeted to the Peruvian population with information regarding national large-scale assessment results
- *Video material*: Videos explaining how to understand findings from national large-scale assessments targeted to the general population
- *Video material for families*: Videos explaining how to provide student support at home in mathematics and reading comprehension and the relevance of mathematics and science in everyday life
- *Photographs*: Photographs taken during assessment workshops, conferences, and press releases
- *Broadcast material*: Miscellaneous files and documents on the use of assessment results and the online platform.

Source: Ministerio de Educación 2019.

Key Ideas

- The national assessment team should agree on the core set of findings and messages that will be communicated in all formats and develop a plan for reporting these findings to different stakeholders and the general public.
- All reports should present well-reasoned, defensible, statistically sound analyses.
- The main report should be timely, with an emphasis on clear, nontechnical communication of high-level results, and should describe the purpose

and context of the assessment, its framework, its relationship with the national curriculum and national learning goals, and its methodology.

- Charts, graphs, and tables can be used to highlight key findings, especially when key findings depend on multiple comparisons across regions, schools, or student subgroups.
- In addition to the main report, many national assessment teams issue technical and thematic summary reports tailored to different audiences.
- Many countries are increasingly taking advantage of technology to publish materials online, which reduces publication costs but may limit access by certain stakeholder groups.
- In addition to reports, television, radio, internet, and other forms of media can be used to communicate results to a wide array of stakeholders.

References

Greaney, Vincent, and Thomas Kellaghan. 2008. *National Assessments of Educational Achievement, Volume 1: Assessing National Achievement Levels in Education.* Washington, DC: World Bank.

Kellaghan, Thomas, Vincent Greaney, and Scott Murray. 2009. *National Assessments of Educational Achievement, Volume 5: Using the Results of a National Assessment of Educational Achievement.* Washington, DC: World Bank.

Ministerio de Educación. 2019. "Oficina de Medición de la Calidad de los Aprendizajes: Evaluación." http://umc.minedu.gob.pe/evaluaciones-y-factores-asociados.

NCERT (National Council of Educational Research and Training). 2015. *What Students of Class V Know and Can Do. A Summary of India's National Achievement Survey, Class V (Cycle 4) 2015.* New Delhi, India: NCERT.

NCERT (National Council of Educational Research and Training). 2017. *NAS 2017: National Achievement Survey, Class III, V and VII. National Report to Inform Policy, Practices and Teaching Learning.* New Delhi, India: NCERT.

Ra, Sungup, Sungsook Kim, and Ki Jong Rhee. 2019. *Developing National Student Assessment Systems for Quality Education. Lessons from the Republic of Korea.* Manila, Philippines: Asian Development Bank.

Chapter 8 WHAT ARE THE MAIN INTERNATIONAL LARGE-SCALE STUDENT ASSESSMENTS?

International large-scale assessments are designed to provide participating countries with feedback on the performance of their education systems within a comparative framework (box 8.1). They are designed to answer questions such as the following:

- How well do students in my education system perform in comparison with those in other education systems?
- What factors are associated with student performance in my education system?
- What factors are associated with student performance across many countries' education systems?
- Are students in my education system performing better or worse over time?

This chapter provides a brief overview of three international large-scale assessments: the Trends in International Mathematics and Science Study (TIMSS), the Progress in International Reading Literacy Study (PIRLS), and the Programme for International Student Assessment (PISA). Annex A (table 8A.1) compares key dimensions of each of these assessments. More detailed information can be found by visiting the official websites or contacting the sponsoring organization for each assessment (included in the reference section of this chapter).

BOX 8.1. How Much Does It Cost to Participate in an International Large-Scale Assessment? Why Participate?

Countries face direct and indirect costs for participating in international large-scale assessments. The cost structure differs for each assessment, and costs are updated in advance of each assessment cycle.

- Direct costs include a base participation fee that covers instrument development and test materials; this base fee may differ, depending on the assessment delivery format (paper- versus computer-based assessment). Additional direct costs may include fees paid for technical support, oversampling populations of interest, and additional analysis of assessment results.
- Indirect costs are mainly related to local resources that countries draw on to implement the assessment: for example, recruitment of test administrators, logistics for assessment implementation, translation of assessment materials, and scoring of open-ended items.

Participating in regional and international large-scale assessments also has benefits. International assessment organizations provide training, tutorials, and workshops to build technical capacity in implementing, scoring, analyzing, and reporting large-scale assessment results. This capacity-building support is particularly useful for countries with limited human resources in their national assessment agencies or with little experience implementing large-scale assessment studies. International assessment organizations also develop publicly available knowledge products, such as online tutorials, user-friendly data analysis tools, and data management files for countries and other stakeholders interested in learning how to analyze large-scale assessment results and report findings.

In addition, countries can use results from these assessments to produce indicators and compare learning progress. Data from most international and regional large-scale assessments are publicly available to policy makers, researchers, and other stakeholders interested in conducting secondary data analyses. Finally, regional and international organizations arrange conferences and other events to promote dialogue and knowledge building in participating countries, which can help countries share experiences and identify common challenges and possible solutions for implementation of large-scale assessments and use of their results.

Websites for each of these international assessment organizations are in the reference section of this chapter. Readers are encouraged to visit these websites for more information about capacity-building training and publicly available tools and materials developed for countries and researchers.

Trends in International Mathematics and Science Study

The International Association for the Evaluation of Educational Achievement oversees TIMSS, which assesses mathematics and science achievement levels of students in grades 4 and 8. This includes assessment of the knowledge of concepts, facts, and procedures; application of this knowledge to familiar real-life scenarios; and ability to reason through complex, multistep problems.

TIMSS was first administered in 1995 and has been administered every four years since: 1999, 2003, 2007, 2011, 2015, and 2019. The number of participating education systems has increased from 45 in 1995 to 64 in 2019.

Because scores from different administrations are expressed on a single scale, countries that have participated in more than one TIMSS cycle can analyze their achievement trends over time (Mullis and Martin 2017).

TIMSS distinguishes between intended, implemented, and attained curriculum. The intended curriculum represents society's goals for teaching and learning as codified in curricula, syllabi, and policy statements and reflected in textbooks, educational resources, and national assessments. The implemented curriculum is how teachers interpret the intended curriculum and make it available to students. The attained curriculum is what students have learned, as inferred from their performance on TIMSS and other assessments.

Table 8.1 summarizes the mathematics and science content and cognitive domains measured in TIMSS 2019. There is some overlap in the content assessed in grades 4 and 8, but there is also a progression in the complexity of what is assessed at each grade level. For instance, the grade 4 mathematics assessment emphasizes numbers more than the grade 8 assessment, which includes more-abstract topics, such as algebra and probability. The cognitive domains are consistent across assessments but with more emphasis on basic cognitive skills in the grade 4 assessments and on more complex cognitive skills in the grade 8 assessments (Mullis and Martin 2017).

The TIMSS assessment frameworks are updated in each assessment cycle to take into account the curricula and learning standards of the participating countries. International experts review potential framework updates. Once updates are approved, the framework is modified, and related assessment content is developed in a consensus-building process among participating countries (Mullis and Martin 2017).

TABLE 8.1. Content and Cognitive Domains Measured in the 2019 Trends in International Mathematics and Science Study

Subject	Grade	Domain content (percentage of assessment devoted to this content)	Cognitive domain
Mathematics	4	• Number (50) • Measurement and geometry (30) • Data (20)	• *Knowing.* The conceptual knowledge, facts, and familiar procedures students need to know. • *Applying.* Students' ability to apply conceptual knowledge to solve familiar real-life problems. • *Reasoning.* Goes beyond the solution of routine problems to include unfamiliar situations, complex contexts, and multistep problems.
	8	• Number (30) • Algebra (30) • Geometry (20) • Data and probability (20)	
Science	4	• Life science (45) • Physical science (35) • Earth science (20)	
	8	• Biology (35) • Chemistry (20) • Physics (25) • Earth science (20)	

Source: Adapted from Mullis and Martin 2017.

As of the most recent assessment cycle, participating countries were able to choose between a pencil-and-paper or computer-based administration format. In 2019, approximately one-half of participating countries chose pencil-and-paper administration, and the other half chose computer-based administration. In general, the trend is toward computer-based administration, which allows the International Association for the Evaluation of Educational Achievement to include more innovative problem-solving and inquiry tasks in the assessment. Computer-based assessments also enable more efficient automated scoring of multiple-choice and some constructed response items, instead of relying solely on human raters to score and record student responses (Mullis and Martin 2017).

Background questionnaires for students, teachers, school principals, parents, and country representatives accompany TIMSS assessments. The student questionnaire collects information on student experiences with and attitudes toward mathematics and science. The questionnaires for teachers and principals gather information on school and classroom resources and instructional approaches. Parents answer a questionnaire focused on contexts for learning at home. Country representatives provide information on content coverage and learning trajectories in the national curriculum (Mullis and Martin 2017).

Map 8.1 shows country participation in TIMSS from 1995 to 2019. Most participating countries are in Europe, Central and East Asia, and the Middle East. Few Latin American or African countries have participated in TIMSS. Australia; England; Hong Kong SAR, China; Hungary; Islamic Republic of Iran; Italy; Japan; Lithuania; New Zealand; Russian Federation; Singapore; Slovenia; the United States; and the Canadian provinces of Ontario and Quebec have participated in all seven TIMSS cycles. The TIMSS website includes historical information about country participation in each TIMSS study cycle.

TIMSS presents findings in terms of the overall score of each participating country; the distribution of achievement within each country, including percentage of students reaching various performance levels; the differences between particular student groups (for example, boys versus girls); and the relative performance in different topic and skill areas.

For example, figure 8.1 shows proficiency level distributions for each country that participated in the grade 4 mathematics assessment for TIMSS 2019. Countries with similar overall scores have quite different distributions of student achievement. This is why it is important to look beyond the overall score when examining a country's results on TIMSS.

TIMSS also presents results in terms of percentages of students in each country reaching various international benchmarks: low, intermediate, high, and advanced. In 2019, only 7 percent of students in grade 4 scored above the advanced international benchmark in mathematics. This benchmark is linked to the capacity to apply mathematical knowledge and reasoning to complex multistep problems and explain one's solution process. At the same time, only 8 percent of students who participated in TIMSS 2019 performed below the lowest benchmark; these students are not able to solve basic arithmetic problems and lack knowledge of fractions, geometry, and measurement. Singapore; Hong Kong SAR, China; and the Republic of Korea had the largest proportion

MAP 8.1. Country Participation in the Trends in International Mathematics and Science Study, 1995–2019

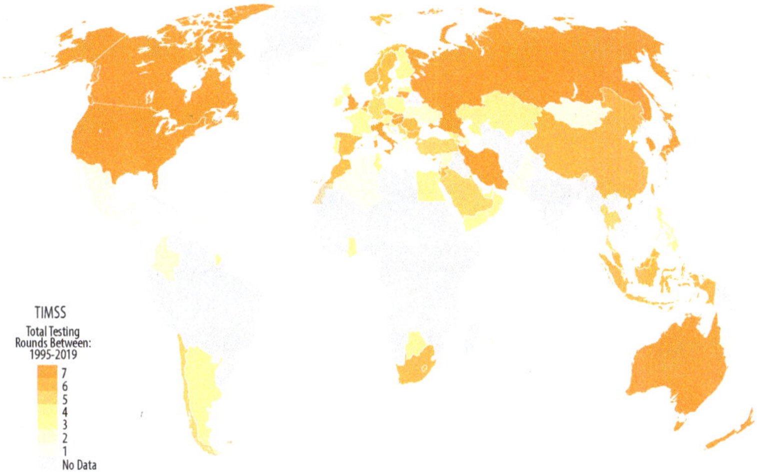

TIMSS
Total Testing Rounds Between: 1995-2019
7
6
5
4
3
2
1
No Data

IBRD 45403 | FEBRUARY 2021

Source: Original compilation for this publication.

Note: Argentina; Belgium; Canada; Hong Kong SAR, China; Russian Federation; Spain; the United Arab Emirates; and the United States have participated at the subnational and national levels.

of students achieving above the highest international benchmark. Twelve countries have increased the proportion of their students reaching the highest international benchmarks between TIMSS 1995 and TIMSS 2019: Australia; Cyprus; England; Hong Kong SAR, China; the Islamic Republic of Iran; Ireland; Japan; Korea; New Zealand; Portugal; Singapore; and the United States (Mullis et al. 2020).

Differences according to sex were minimal in most countries participating in the TIMSS 2019 assessment in grade 4. However, in some countries, girls performed significantly better than boys (for example, Oman, Pakistan, the Philippines, Saudi Arabia, and South Africa); in others, boys performed significantly better than girls (for example, Canada, Cyprus, Portugal, and Spain) (Mullis et al. 2020).

Many countries have used findings from TIMSS (box 8.2) and other International Association for the Evaluation of Educational Achievement assessments (box 8.3) to inform their education policy and planning (box 8.4).

Progress in International Reading Literacy Study

The International Association for the Evaluation of Educational Achievement also oversees PIRLS, which is administered to students in grade 4 (Mullis and Martin 2015). The first PIRLS was administered in 2001, and it has been

FIGURE 8.1. Trends in International Mathematics and Science Study 2019 Grade 4 Performance, According to International Benchmarks of Mathematics Achievement

Percentages of Students Reaching International Benchmarks: ● Advanced ● High ● Intermediate ● Low (scale 0, 25, 50, 75, 100)

Country or Economy	Advanced Benchmark (625)	High Benchmark (550)	Intermediate Benchmark (475)	Low Benchmark (400)
[3]Singapore	54 (2.2)	84 (1.5)	96 (0.7)	99 (0.3)
[†]Hong Kong SAR, China	38 (1.9)	78 (1.6)	96 (0.7)	100 (0.2)
Korea, Rep. of	37 (1.4)	77 (1.2)	95 (0.5)	99 (0.2)
Taiwan, China	37 (1.3)	78 (1.1)	96 (0.5)	100 (0.2)
Japan	33 (1.3)	74 (0.9)	95 (0.4)	99 (0.2)
[†]Northern Ireland	26 (1.4)	60 (1.4)	85 (1.1)	96 (0.6)
[2]England	21 (1.4)	53 (1.5)	83 (1.2)	96 (0.5)
[2]Russian Federation	20 (1.6)	61 (1.9)	91 (1.0)	99 (0.3)
Ireland	15 (1.0)	52 (1.4)	84 (1.0)	97 (0.5)
[2]Turkey (5)	15 (1.3)	43 (1.8)	70 (1.7)	88 (1.3)
[2†]United States	14 (0.8)	46 (1.3)	77 (1.1)	93 (0.6)
[2]Lithuania	13 (1.1)	48 (1.6)	81 (1.1)	96 (0.6)
[†]Norway (5)	13 (0.9)	48 (1.3)	82 (1.2)	97 (0.6)
Cyprus	12 (0.9)	42 (1.6)	77 (1.3)	95 (0.6)
[2]Latvia	11 (0.9)	50 (1.7)	85 (1.2)	98 (0.6)
Finland	11 (0.8)	42 (1.3)	78 (1.2)	95 (0.6)
Czech Republic	10 (1.0)	42 (1.5)	78 (1.3)	96 (0.6)
Australia	10 (0.9)	36 (1.2)	70 (1.3)	90 (1.0)
Austria	9 (0.7)	45 (1.4)	84 (1.1)	98 (0.4)
Hungary	9 (0.8)	39 (1.4)	74 (1.3)	93 (0.8)
[2]Portugal	9 (0.7)	39 (1.6)	74 (1.2)	95 (0.7)
[†]Denmark	8 (0.9)	37 (1.3)	75 (1.0)	95 (0.5)
[†]Belgium (Flemish)	8 (0.5)	40 (1.2)	80 (1.2)	97 (0.4)
Bulgaria	8 (0.6)	37 (1.7)	71 (1.9)	90 (1.5)
Poland	8 (0.8)	36 (1.4)	73 (1.4)	93 (0.6)
Azerbaijan	8 (0.6)	36 (1.3)	72 (1.5)	92 (0.8)
Sweden	8 (0.8)	36 (1.7)	74 (1.4)	94 (0.7)
[■]Netherlands	7 (0.9)	44 (1.7)	84 (1.1)	98 (0.4)
[2]Serbia	7 (0.7)	32 (1.4)	68 (1.5)	89 (1.1)
United Arab Emirates	7 (0.3)	26 (0.6)	53 (0.8)	78 (0.7)
[12]Canada	6 (0.6)	32 (1.0)	69 (0.9)	92 (0.6)
[2]New Zealand	6 (0.5)	25 (1.2)	56 (1.3)	83 (0.9)
Germany	6 (0.6)	36 (1.5)	75 (1.2)	96 (0.6)
Albania	5 (0.6)	26 (1.4)	62 (1.8)	86 (1.3)
[2]Slovak Republic	5 (0.7)	31 (1.7)	71 (1.7)	91 (1.2)
Malta	5 (0.5)	32 (0.9)	69 (0.8)	91 (0.6)
North Macedonia	5 (0.8)	21 (1.8)	52 (2.4)	78 (1.7)
[2]Kazakhstan	5 (0.6)	29 (1.5)	71 (1.4)	95 (0.6)
Bahrain	4 (0.4)	21 (1.0)	54 (1.2)	81 (1.0)
Italy	4 (0.5)	30 (1.5)	73 (1.3)	95 (0.5)
Croatia	4 (0.6)	28 (1.3)	70 (1.5)	95 (0.7)
Spain	4 (0.4)	27 (0.9)	65 (1.3)	91 (1.0)
France	3 (0.5)	21 (1.2)	57 (1.6)	85 (1.2)
Oman	3 (0.8)	12 (1.3)	33 (1.5)	62 (1.3)
[†]Georgia	3 (0.4)	20 (1.4)	56 (2.0)	84 (1.4)
Armenia	3 (0.5)	23 (1.4)	64 (1.6)	92 (0.7)
Qatar	2 (0.4)	14 (1.2)	40 (1.6)	70 (1.4)
Iran, Islamic Rep. of	2 (0.3)	13 (1.0)	39 (1.6)	68 (1.5)
Montenegro	1 (0.2)	11 (0.7)	43 (0.9)	76 (0.9)
Morocco	1 (0.8)	6 (1.1)	18 (1.4)	43 (1.7)
South Africa (5)	1 (0.2)	5 (0.5)	16 (1.1)	37 (1.5)
[2]Saudi Arabia	1 (0.2)	6 (0.6)	23 (1.2)	51 (1.4)
Kuwait	1 (0.2)	6 (0.9)	21 (1.6)	47 (1.8)
[2]Kosovo	1 (0.2)	8 (0.8)	37 (1.5)	73 (1.4)
Chile	1 (0.1)	7 (0.6)	33 (1.4)	70 (1.5)
Bosnia and Herzegovina	1 (0.2)	9 (0.7)	40 (1.5)	76 (1.1)
[2ψ]Pakistan	0 (0.1)	1 (0.3)	8 (1.5)	27 (4.7)
[2ψ]Philippines	0 (0.1)	1 (0.2)	6 (0.8)	19 (1.8)
International Median	7	34	71	92
Benchmarking Participants				
Moscow City, Russian Fed.	31 (1.5)	77 (1.4)	96 (0.5)	100 (0.2)
[2]Dubai, UAE	16 (0.9)	50 (0.9)	80 (0.8)	95 (0.5)
Quebec, Canada	8 (0.8)	41 (1.4)	80 (1.3)	97 (0.5)
[2]Ontario, Canada	7 (1.0)	32 (1.8)	68 (1.6)	92 (0.9)
Madrid, Spain	5 (0.5)	33 (1.2)	74 (1.5)	96 (0.6)
Abu Dhabi, UAE	3 (0.2)	15 (0.6)	37 (1.0)	64 (1.1)

Source: Mullis et al. 2020.

Note: ψ indicates reservations about reliability because the percentage of students with achievement too low for estimation exceeds 15% but does not exceed 25%. ( ) Standard errors appear in parentheses. Because of rounding some results may appear inconsistent. For additional information on these and other symbols shown in the figure, please consult appendices B.2 and B.5 of the TIMSS 2019 report.

BOX 8.2. Sample of Trends in International Mathematics and Science Study 2019 Key Findings

- Higher scores in mathematics and science were associated with more educational resources and greater parental support for learning at home.
- Better performance on the grade 4 mathematics assessment was related to longer enrollment in preprimary education (three years or more).
- Grade 4 and 8 students enrolled in schools with more learning materials and learning resources tended to have higher scores in mathematics.
- Grade 4 and 8 students reporting a more positive sense of school belonging tended to have higher average scores in mathematics, whereas students that experienced bullying tended to have lower average scores.
- Student attendance had a positive effect on student performance. Students who expressed having never or almost never been absent from school tended to have higher scores in mathematics and science.

Source: Mullis et al. 2020.

BOX 8.3. Other Trends in International Mathematics and Science Study Assessments

Trends in International Mathematics and Science Study (TIMSS) Advanced assesses mathematics and science knowledge and skills of students at the end of secondary school who are interested in pursuing a career in science, technology, engineering, or mathematics. It is administered less frequently than the main TIMSS assessments in grades 4 and 8. TIMSS Advanced covers concepts and skills in mathematics (algebra, calculus, geometry) and physics (mechanics and thermodynamics, electricity and magnetism, wave phenomena, atomic and nuclear physics). It has been administered in 1995, 2008, and 2015 (Mullis and Martin 2017).

TIMSS Numeracy is a less difficult version of the TIMSS grade 4 mathematics assessment. Available since 2015, it is designed for countries where the majority of grade 4 students are still developing foundational mathematics skills. Countries can decide to participate in TIMSS, TIMSS Numeracy, or both, depending on their context. TIMSS Numeracy scores are expressed on the same scale as the main TIMSS assessments, so countries participating in this assessment do not require a separate results report.

Source: Mullis and Martin 2017.

BOX 8.4. Experience of the Russian Federation with the Trends in International Mathematics and Science Study

The Russian Federation participated in the Trends in International Mathematics and Science Study (TIMSS) in 2003, 2007, 2011, 2015, and 2019. Because TIMSS scaled scores permit achievement levels to be tracked over time, it is possible to determine that the Russian Federation achieved a large increase in its average grade 4 mathematics score on TIMSS between 2003 (average 532 points) and 2019 (average 567 points).

During this time, the Russian Federation invested in developing a robust national system to evaluate the quality of education. Reforms included the following:

- Introduction of new federal educational standards in 2011 for primary schools and 2015 for basic schools. The new standards emphasized competency-based curriculum development and student achievement in personal, metacognitive, and academic areas.
- Creation of an independent national examinations system, the Unified State Examination, in 2009. Results are used to certify basic education and university entrance admissions.
- Introduction of an independent system for evaluating the quality of education in schools. The Ministry of Education and Science developed special recommendations for conducting independent evaluations and using the results.

At the same time, policy makers and other stakeholders in the Russian Federation have used TIMSS results to do the following:

- Inform stakeholders about the country's global standing in mathematics and science
- Perform secondary analysis and identify factors linked to student achievement
- Develop new state learning standards
- Develop new master's degree programs in educational measurement and evaluation.

Source: Bolotov et al. 2013; Kovaleva and Krasnianskaia 2016.

administered every five years since (2006, 2011, 2016), with the next PIRLS scheduled to occur in 2021. Similar to TIMSS, the assessment framework is updated each cycle to incorporate information about the national curricula and learning standards of participating countries. The process of updating the assessment framework provides countries with an opportunity to reflect on their educational policies and curricula and how to improve reading achievement.

The PIRLS 2016 assessment framework is built around two of the main purposes of student reading activities inside and outside of school: for literary experience and to acquire and use information. The framework also incorporates four types of cognitive processes associated with reading: retrieval of explicitly stated information, formulation of direct inferences, interpretation and integration of information, and text content evaluation and criticism (Mullis and Martin 2015). In the PIRLS 2016 framework, reading literacy is defined as: "the ability to understand and use those written language forms required by society and/or valued by the individual. Readers can construct meaning from texts in a variety of forms. They read to learn, to participate in communities of readers in school and everyday life, and for enjoyment" (Mullis and Martin 2015, pp. 12).

PIRLS administers background questionnaires to students to gather sociodemographic information and measure their attitudes toward reading and learning. Questionnaires are also administered to parents, teachers, and principals to acquire information about additional factors that affect student reading comprehension.

The number of countries participating in PIRLS has grown from 35 in 2001 to 50 in 2016. Map 8.2 shows the countries that participated in PIRLS between 2001 and 2016. Similar to TIMSS, most participating countries have been from Europe, Central and East Asia, and the Middle East. Very few Latin American or African countries have participated. The PIRLS website and reports include historical information about country participation in each PIRLS cycle.

PIRLS presents findings in terms of the overall score of each participating country; the distribution of achievement within each country, including the percentage of students reaching various performance levels; the differences between student groups (for example, boys versus girls); and the relative performance in different skill areas (boxes 8.5, 8.6, and 8.7).

For example, figure 8.2 shows the distribution of student achievement expressed in proficiency levels for each country that participated in PIRLS 2016. Similar to the TIMSS results, countries with similar overall scores have different distributions of student achievement. PIRLS scores are classified according to four international performance benchmarks: advanced, high, intermediate, and low. Scoring above the advanced benchmark denotes the ability to interpret

MAP 8.2. Country Participation in the Progress in International Reading Literacy Study, 2001–16

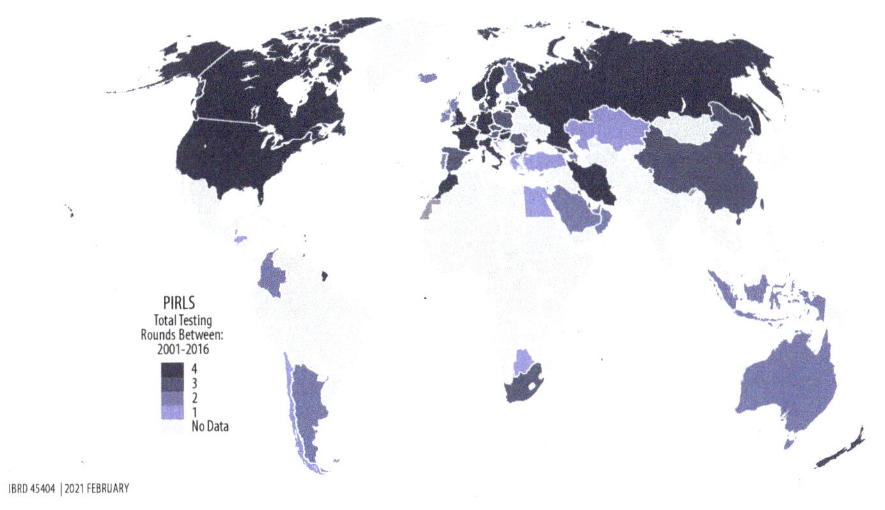

Source: Original compilation based on PIRLS.

Note: Argentina; Belgium; Canada; Hong Kong SAR, China; Macao SAR, China; Malta; Russian Federation; Spain; the United Arab Emirates ; and the United States have participated at the subnational and national level.

BOX 8.5. Sample of Progress in International Reading Literacy Study 2016 Key Findings

- Students with parents reporting greater enjoyment of reading had higher scores than those whose parents had a less positive attitude toward reading.
- Social factors, such as school social climate, were associated with differences in scores; students who reported a higher sense of school belonging also tended to have higher reading scores.
- Students enrolled in schools with more learning materials and learning resources tended to have higher reading scores.
- Students who reported being regularly bullied had lower average scores.
- Students who reported arriving at school feeling hungry every day had lower reading scores than those who never arrived feeling hungry at school.

Source: Mullis et al. 2017.

BOX 8.6. Other Progress in International Reading Literacy Study Assessments

The International Association for the Evaluation of Educational Achievement has developed two additional reading assessments to complement the Progress in International Reading Literacy Study (PIRLS): PIRLS Literacy and ePIRLS. Since the 2016 PIRLS cycle, countries have had the opportunity to participate in these assessments in addition to, or instead of, the standard PIRLS assessment.

The PIRLS Literacy assessment is a less difficult version of PIRLS; it includes shorter reading passages and a higher proportion of items requiring the identification and retrieval of explicitly stated information in the text. PIRLS Literacy results are reported on the same scale as PIRLS to allow for cross-country comparisons.

ePIRLS is a computer-based reading assessment designed to integrate reading comprehension and twenty-first century digital skills. Students engage in an internet browser simulation, with authentic school-like assignments and websites with information in several digital formats. A teacher avatar provides guidance and asks questions about information presented on the screen

Source: Mullis and Martin 2015.

and integrate complex information from different parts of a text and to consider the author's point of view. In 2016, Singapore and the Russian Federation had the highest percentage of students scoring above the advanced benchmark. Only 4 percent of students participating in PIRLS 2016 received scores below the low benchmark, which reflects the inability to locate and retrieve explicitly stated information or make straightforward inferences from simple literary and informational texts (Mullis et al. 2017).

Girls outperformed boys in most countries; the average advantage for girls across the 50 countries participating in PIRLS 2016 was 19 points. The only countries with similar reading scores for girls and boys were Macao SAR, China; and Portugal (Mullis et al. 2017).

Table 8.2 categorizes the items used in PIRLS, PIRLS Literacy, and ePIRLS according to reading purpose and process; the proportion of items measuring each of the different reading comprehension processes differs according to assessment.

BOX 8.7. Georgia's Experience with the Progress in International Reading Literacy Study

Georgia participated in the 2006, 2011, and 2016 rounds of the Progress in International Reading Literacy Study (PIRLS). PIRLS results from 2006 and 2011 were influential in motivating policy makers to identify priorities for teacher professional development and in informing curricular reform by the National Teacher Professional Development Center. Specifically, the PIRLS results provided useful inputs for an initiative to develop handbooks to help teachers with reading instruction in the primary grades. The handbooks produced were as follows:

- *How to Teach Reading* served as a practical guide to the latest pedagogical methods for teaching reading skills in the primary grades.
- *Let's Learn to Read* complemented *How to Teach Reading* and focused on how to promote reading with comprehension among students enrolled in primary grade classrooms. It included a collection of stories for children, along with classroom quizzes, for teachers to assess reading comprehension.
- *PIRLS 2006 Results* described Georgian student performance on the PIRLS 2006 assessment and provided details on where students were strong in their reading skills and where they required further support

Source: Mullis et al. 2012.

TABLE 8.2. Proportion of Items in Progress in International Reading Literacy Study (PIRLS) Assessments According to Reading Purpose and Reading Comprehension Process

	PIRLS (%)	PIRLS Literacy (%)	ePIRLS (%)
Purpose of reading			
Have a literary experience	50	50	0
Acquire and use information	50	50	100
Reading comprehension process			
Focus on and retrieve explicitly stated information	20	50	20
Make straightforward inferences	30	25	30
Interpret and integrate ideas and information	30	25	30
Evaluate and critique content and textual elements	20		20

Source: Adapted from Mullis and Martin 2015.

FIGURE 8.2. Progress in International Reading Literacy Study 2016 Performance, According to International Benchmarks of Reading Achievement

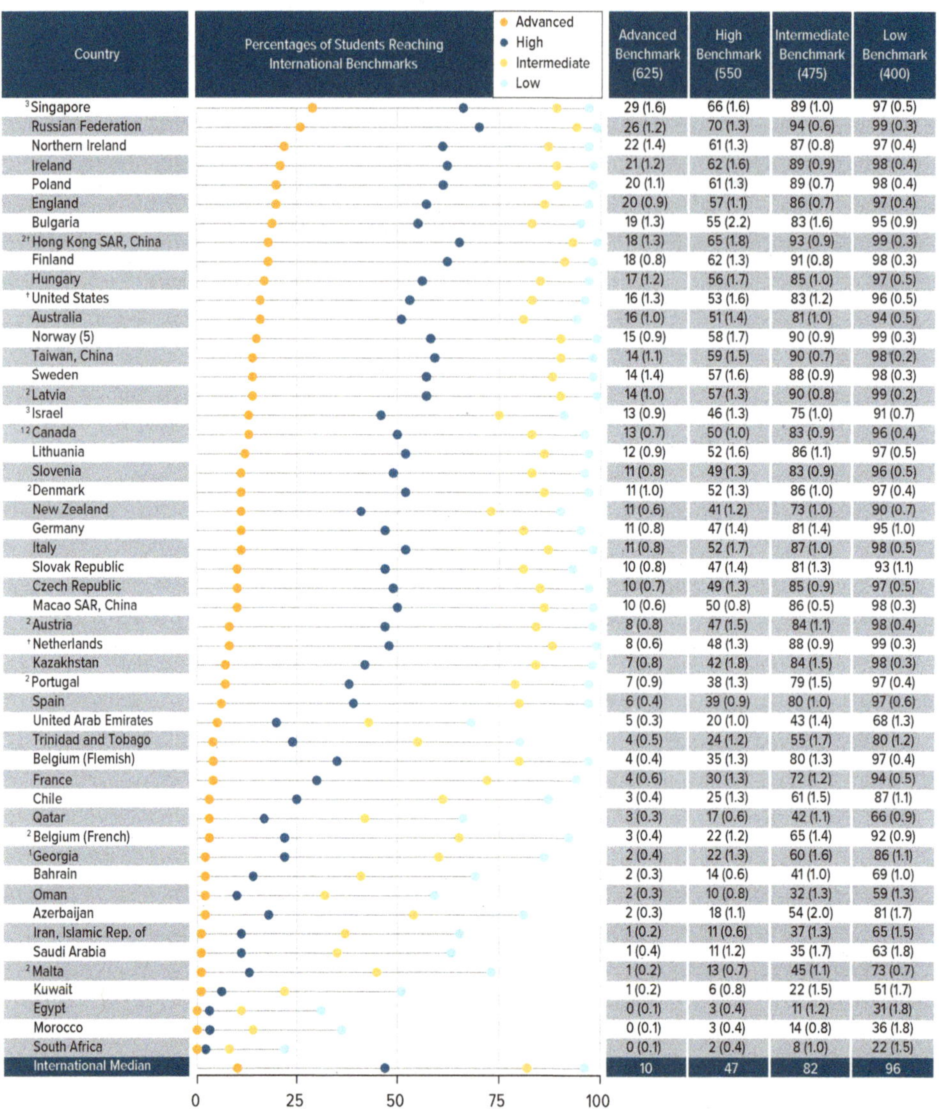

Country	Advanced Benchmark (625)	High Benchmark (550	Intermediate Benchmark (475)	Low Benchmark (400)
[3] Singapore	29 (1.6)	66 (1.6)	89 (1.0)	97 (0.5)
Russian Federation	26 (1.2)	70 (1.3)	94 (0.6)	99 (0.3)
Northern Ireland	22 (1.4)	61 (1.3)	87 (0.8)	97 (0.4)
Ireland	21 (1.2)	62 (1.6)	89 (0.9)	98 (0.4)
Poland	20 (1.1)	61 (1.3)	89 (0.7)	98 (0.4)
England	20 (0.9)	57 (1.1)	86 (0.7)	97 (0.4)
Bulgaria	19 (1.3)	55 (2.2)	83 (1.6)	95 (0.9)
[2†] Hong Kong SAR, China	18 (1.3)	65 (1.8)	93 (0.9)	99 (0.3)
Finland	18 (0.8)	62 (1.3)	91 (0.8)	98 (0.3)
Hungary	17 (1.2)	56 (1.7)	85 (1.0)	97 (0.5)
[†] United States	16 (1.3)	53 (1.6)	83 (1.2)	96 (0.5)
Australia	16 (1.0)	51 (1.4)	81 (1.0)	94 (0.5)
Norway (5)	15 (0.9)	58 (1.7)	90 (0.9)	99 (0.3)
Taiwan, China	14 (1.1)	59 (1.5)	90 (0.7)	98 (0.2)
Sweden	14 (1.4)	57 (1.6)	88 (0.9)	98 (0.3)
[2] Latvia	14 (1.0)	57 (1.3)	90 (0.8)	99 (0.2)
[3] Israel	13 (0.9)	46 (1.3)	75 (1.0)	91 (0.7)
[1,2] Canada	13 (0.7)	50 (1.0)	83 (0.9)	96 (0.4)
Lithuania	12 (0.9)	52 (1.6)	86 (1.1)	97 (0.5)
Slovenia	11 (0.8)	49 (1.3)	83 (0.9)	96 (0.5)
[2] Denmark	11 (1.0)	52 (1.3)	86 (1.0)	97 (0.4)
New Zealand	11 (0.6)	41 (1.2)	73 (1.0)	90 (0.7)
Germany	11 (0.8)	47 (1.4)	81 (1.4)	95 (1.0)
Italy	11 (0.8)	52 (1.7)	87 (1.0)	98 (0.5)
Slovak Republic	10 (0.8)	47 (1.4)	81 (1.3)	93 (1.1)
Czech Republic	10 (0.7)	49 (1.3)	85 (0.9)	97 (0.5)
Macao SAR, China	10 (0.6)	50 (0.8)	86 (0.5)	98 (0.3)
[2] Austria	8 (0.8)	47 (1.5)	84 (1.1)	98 (0.4)
[†] Netherlands	8 (0.6)	48 (1.3)	88 (0.9)	99 (0.3)
Kazakhstan	7 (0.8)	42 (1.8)	84 (1.5)	98 (0.3)
[2] Portugal	7 (0.9)	38 (1.3)	79 (1.5)	97 (0.4)
Spain	6 (0.4)	39 (0.9)	80 (1.0)	97 (0.6)
United Arab Emirates	5 (0.3)	20 (1.0)	43 (1.4)	68 (1.3)
Trinidad and Tobago	4 (0.5)	24 (1.2)	55 (1.7)	80 (1.2)
Belgium (Flemish)	4 (0.4)	35 (1.3)	80 (1.3)	97 (0.4)
France	4 (0.6)	30 (1.3)	72 (1.2)	94 (0.5)
Chile	3 (0.4)	25 (1.3)	61 (1.5)	87 (1.1)
Qatar	3 (0.3)	17 (0.6)	42 (1.1)	66 (0.9)
[2] Belgium (French)	3 (0.4)	22 (1.2)	65 (1.4)	92 (0.9)
[1] Georgia	2 (0.4)	22 (1.3)	60 (1.6)	86 (1.1)
Bahrain	2 (0.3)	14 (0.6)	41 (1.0)	69 (1.0)
Oman	2 (0.3)	10 (0.8)	32 (1.3)	59 (1.3)
Azerbaijan	2 (0.3)	18 (1.1)	54 (2.0)	81 (1.7)
Iran, Islamic Rep. of	1 (0.2)	11 (0.6)	37 (1.3)	65 (1.5)
Saudi Arabia	1 (0.4)	11 (1.2)	35 (1.7)	63 (1.8)
[2] Malta	1 (0.2)	13 (0.7)	45 (1.1)	73 (0.7)
Kuwait	1 (0.2)	6 (0.8)	22 (1.5)	51 (1.7)
Egypt	0 (0.1)	3 (0.4)	11 (1.2)	31 (1.8)
Morocco	0 (0.1)	3 (0.4)	14 (0.8)	36 (1.8)
South Africa	0 (0.1)	2 (0.4)	8 (1.0)	22 (1.5)
International Median	10	47	82	96

Source: Mullis et al. 2017.

Note: Please consult appendices C.1 and C.4 of the PIRLS 2016 report for target population coverage notes 1, 2, and 3, sampling guidelines, and sampling participation note †. ( ) Standard errors appear in parentheses. Because of rounding, some results may appear inconsistent.

Programme for International Student Assessment

The Organisation for Economic Co-operation and Development (OECD) started the Programme for International Student Assessment (PISA) in 2000 to collect information on student achievement near the end of compulsory schooling. Since then, the assessment has been administered every three years: 2003, 2006, 2009, 2012, 2015, and 2018. The next PISA assessment was planned for 2021, but its final administration has been postponed to 2022 because of the coronavirus pandemic. PISA is administered to 15-year-olds to assess their knowledge and skills in reading literacy, mathematics literacy, and science literacy, all of which are considered essential for participation in social and economic life. In addition to these core subject areas, more recent PISA cycles have included topics such as collaborative problem solving, financial literacy, and global competence (OECD 2019) (see also box 8.8).

The PISA 2018 assessment framework defines the three main subjects measured in the assessment, as follows:

- *Reading literacy*. Capacity to understand, use, evaluate, reflect on, and engage with texts to achieve goals, develop knowledge and potential, and participate in society.
- *Mathematics literacy*. Capacity to formulate, use, and interpret mathematics in a variety of contexts; includes reasoning mathematically and using mathematical concepts, procedures, facts, and tools to describe, explain, and predict phenomena.

BOX 8.8. Other Programme for International Student Assessment Assessments

The Organisation for Economic Co-operation and Development (OECD) started the Programme for International Student Assessment (PISA) for Development (PISA-D) pilot in 2014 to create an accessible assessment for a wider range of low- and middle-income countries. Eight countries participated in the pilot: Bhutan, Cambodia, Ecuador, Guatemala, Honduras, Paraguay, Senegal, and Zambia. The instruments used in this pilot are now being offered as an option to countries that sign up for the regular PISA. The instruments draw on the same framework as the regular PISA tests but target performance at lower levels of proficiency.

The PISA-D pilot included a paper-based assessment for students in school and a tablet-based assessment for youth no longer enrolled in school. The in-school assessment covered reading, mathematics, and science; the out-of-school instrument focused on reading and mathematics. PISA-D also collected contextual information to determine which factors contribute to achievement on the test. Participating countries underwent a capacity needs analysis exercise that the OECD used to design a capacity-building plan tailored to their needs. The capacity-building options designed for countries participating in the PISA-D pilot have been made available to countries participating in the regular PISA, including capacity building and support for key assessment tasks, such as sampling, adaptation of measurement tools, data management, data analysis, and results reporting.

Source: OECD 2018.

BOX 8.9. Translation and Adaptation of International Large-Scale Assessments

Every Trends in International Mathematics and Science Study (TIMSS), Progress in International Reading Literacy Study (PIRLS), and Programme for International Student Assessment (PISA) exercise involves the participation of countries from around the globe. Thus, questions related to translation and adaptation of these assessments commonly arise, particularly for countries interested in taking part in any of these international large-scale assessments for the first time.

The TIMSS and PIRLS International Study Center at Boston College produces the international versions of these assessments and related materials in English, along with guidelines for translation and adaptation. National country representatives for each participating country are responsible for the translation of all materials into their languages of instruction and the adaptation to their cultural context while maintaining international comparability. External experts review each assessment translation and adaptation to verify the accuracy and comparability in the translation process.

Two international versions of the PISA test and related materials are produced—one in English and one in French. Countries are required to perform two independent translations of either international version of the assessment into their official language of instruction. External reviewers verify the accuracy, equivalence, and fidelity of the translation and identify any discrepancies. After that, experts known as *reconcilers* produce a final translated assessment by reconciling any discrepancies between the two independent translations. Finally, subject matter experts review the materials for precision in the terminology and content.

Sources: Mullis et al. 2017; OECD 2018.

- *Science literacy.* Ability to engage with science-related topics and with the ideas of science as a reflective citizen. A scientifically literate person is willing to engage in reasoned discourse about science and technology, which requires the ability to explain phenomena scientifically, evaluate and design scientific inquiry, and interpret data and evidence scientifically (OECD 2019).

Each assessment cycle emphasizes one of the three core domains: reading, mathematics, and science. In 2018, the emphasis was on reading literacy, but mathematics literacy and science literacy were also assessed. In 2015, science received the greatest emphasis. In PISA 2022, mathematics will receive greater emphasis than the other two subject areas.

In addition to the assessment, students are asked to complete a background questionnaire focused on their home context, attitudes to learning, and learning experiences at school. School principals also complete a questionnaire on school management and the school learning environment. In some countries, an elective questionnaire was administered to teachers to gather additional information about instructional practices in the classroom. An elective questionnaire was also given to parents to determine their involvement in their children's school and learning. Some countries administer additional questionnaires measuring student familiarity with computers, their expectations for further education, and their well-being (OECD 2019).

For most countries, the PISA tests are administered on the computer, although paper-based assessments are available for countries in which students do not have widespread access to computers. Unlike other international large-scale assessments, the computer-based PISA test is adaptive, so students are assigned blocks of items at their level of ability, depending on their performance on preceding item blocks (OECD 2019).

The number of countries participating in PISA has increased from 43 in the first assessment cycle to 79 in 2018 (OECD 2019). Map 8.3 shows the countries that participated in PISA 2018 and in previous years. Similar to TIMSS and PIRLS, many of the countries are from Europe, Central and East Asia, and the Middle East; however, unlike TIMSS and PIRLS, there are many countries from Latin America and the Caribbean.

PISA presents findings in terms of the overall score of each participating country; the distribution of achievement within each country, including the percentage of students reaching different performance levels; the differences between particular student groups (for example, boys versus girls); and the relative performance in different topic or skill areas.

Figure 8.3 presents PISA 2018 mean scores according to subject and country. Students from four Chinese provinces (Beijing, Jiangsu, Shanghai, and Zhejiang) and Singapore had the highest average achievement on the three PISA assessments, followed by students from Macao SAR, China; and Hong Kong SAR, China.

MAP 8.3. Country Participation in the Programme for International Student Assessment, 2000–18

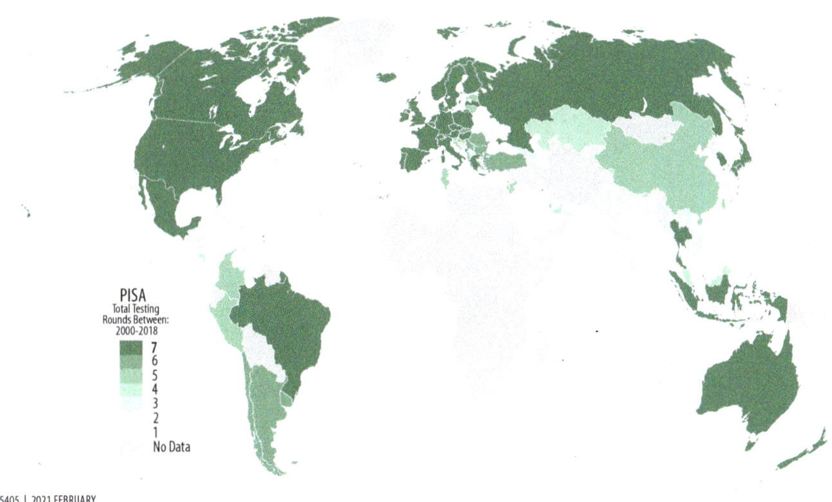

Source: Original compilation based on PISA.

Note: Some countries have participated at the subnational and national level in Programme for International Student Assessment (PISA): Argentina; Azerbaijan; China; Hong Kong SAR, China; India; Macao SAR, China; United Arab Emirates, United States; and Venezuela, RB.

FIGURE 8.3. Programme for International Student Assessment 2018 Distribution of Average Reading, Mathematics, and Science Scores

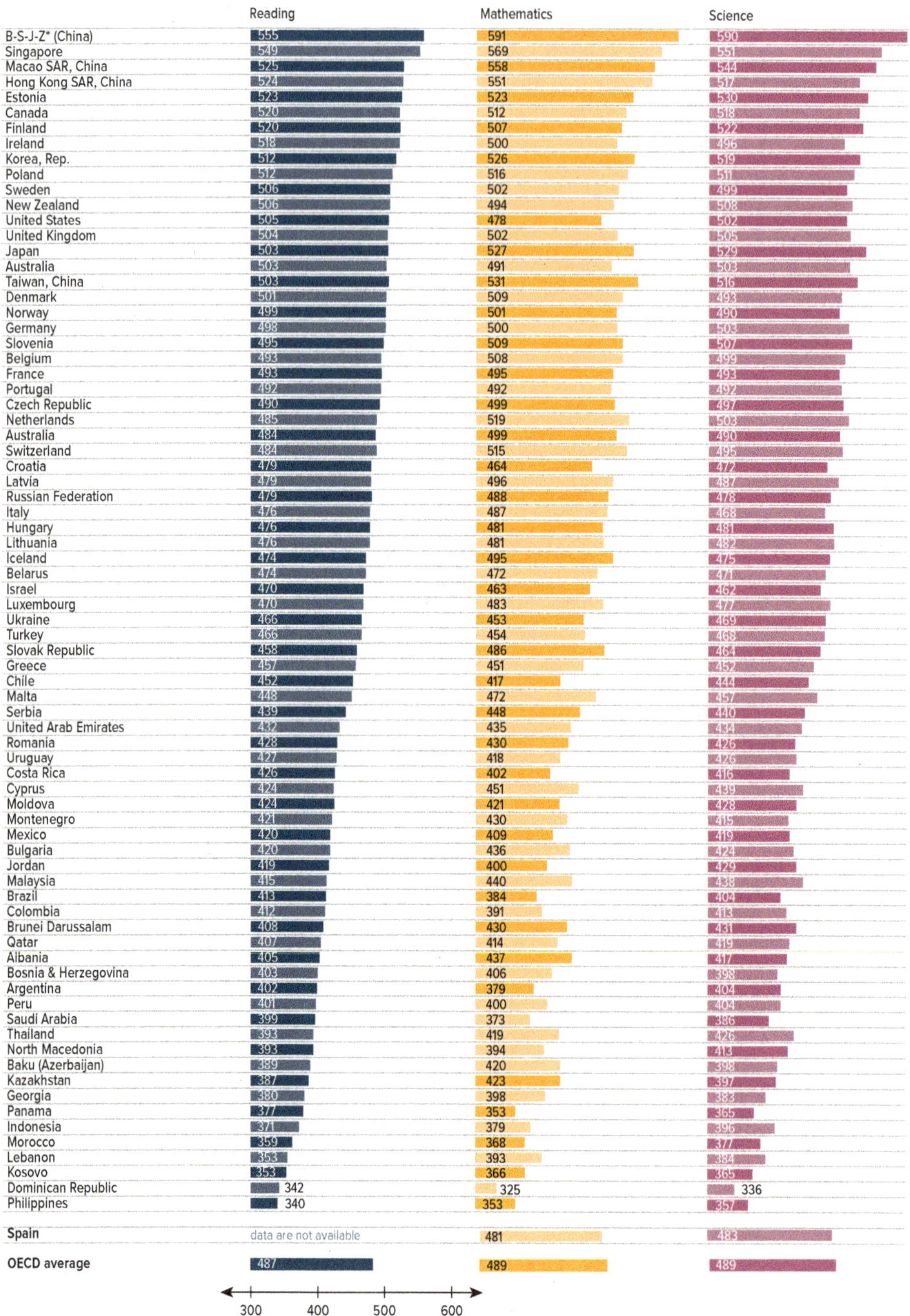

Source: OECD 2019.

Note: B-S-J-Z* stands for Beijing, Jiangsu, Shanghai, and Zhejiang provinces in China.

Of OECD countries, Estonia had the best average performance in reading and science, and the Republic of Korea outperformed all other countries in mathematics. Other top-achieving countries were Canada, Finland, and Ireland.

PISA scores from different assessment cycles are calculated on the same scale so that countries can monitor achievement trends over time. The average performance of students from Albania, Peru, and Qatar improved considerably (OECD 2019).

Reading was the main subject assessed in PISA 2018. Figure 8.4 shows that girls outperformed boys in reading in all participating countries but that the gender differences in mathematics were much smaller. The smallest gender gaps in reading were found in Argentina, Chile, China, Colombia, Costa Rica, Mexico, Panama, and Peru; the largest gaps were found in Finland, Jordan, the Republic of North Macedonia, Qatar, Saudi Arabia, and the United Arab Emirates.

FIGURE 8.4. Programme for International Student Assessment 2018 Gender Gap in Reading and Mathematics Performance

Source: OECD 2019.

Note: B-S-J-Z* stands for Beijing, Jiangsu, Shanghai, and Zhejiang provinces in China.

Annex 8A. Overview of Key Features

TABLE 8A.1. Key Features of International and Regional Large-Scale Assessments

Assessment	Target grades or age	Main subject areas	Organization	Years	Participating regions
Programme for International Student Assessment	15 years	Reading, mathematics, science	Organisation for Economic Co-operation and Development	2000, 2003, 2006, 2009, 2012, 2015, 2018	Global
Trends in International Mathematics and Science Study	Grades 4, 8	Mathematics, science	International Association for the Evaluation of Educational Achievement	1995, 1999, 2003, 2007, 2011, 2015, 2019	Global
Progress in International Reading Literacy Study	Grade 4	Reading	International Association for the Evaluation of Educational Achievement	2001, 2006, 2011, 2016	Global
Latin American Laboratory for Assessment of the Quality of Education	Grades 3, 6	Literacy, mathematics, science	United Nations Educational, Scientific and Cultural Organization—Oficina Regional de Educación para América Latina y el Caribe	1997, 2006, 2013, 2019	Latin America
Program for the Analysis of Education Systems	Grades 2, 6	Reading, mathematics	La Conférence des ministres de l'Éducation des États et gouvernements de la Francophonie	Every year between 1993 and 2010, 2014, 2019	Francophone Africa; select countries in East Asia in the past
Southern and Eastern Africa Consortium for Monitoring Educational Quality	Grade 6	Reading, mathematics, health knowledge	Southern and Eastern Africa Consortium for Monitoring Educational Quality	1999, 2004, 2011, 2014	Anglophone Africa
Pacific Islands Literacy and Numeracy Assessment	Grades 4, 6	Numeracy, literacy	Pacific Community	2012, 2015, 2018	Pacific Islands
Southeast Asia Primary Learning Metrics	Grade 5	Literacy, mathematics, global citizenship	Southeast Asian Ministers of Education Organization Secretariat and United Nations Children's Fund	2019	Southeast Asia

References

Bolotov, Viktor, Galina Kovaleva, Marina Pinskaya, and Igor Valdman. 2013. *Developing the Enabling Context for Student Assessment in Russia*. Washington, DC: World Bank Group.

Kovaleva, Galina, and Klara Krasnianskaia. 2016. "Russian Federation." In *TIMSS 2015 Encyclopedia: Education Policy and Curriculum in Mathematics and Science,* edited by Ina V. S. Mullis, Michael O. Martin, Shirley Goh, and Kerry Cotter. http://timssandpirls.bc.edu/timss2015/encyclopedia/countries/russian-federation/.

Mullis, Ina V. S., and Michael O. Martin, eds. 2015. *PIRLS 2016 Assessment Framework* (2nd ed.). Boston, MA: TIMSS and PIRLS International Study Center. http://timssandpirls.bc.edu/pirls2016/framework.html.

Mullis, Ina V. S., and Michael O. Martin, eds. 2017. *TIMSS 2019 Assessment Frameworks*. Boston, MA: TIMSS and PIRLS International Study Center. http://timssandpirls.bc.edu/timss2019/frameworks/.

Mullis, Ina V. S., Michael O. Martin, Pierre Foy, and Martin Hooper. 2017. *PIRLS 2016 International Results in Reading*. Boston, MA: TIMSS and PIRLS International Study Center. http://timssandpirls.bc.edu/pirls2016/international-results/.

Mullis, Ina V. S., Michael O. Martin, Pierre Foy, Dana L. Kelly, and Bethany Fishbein. 2020. *TIMSS 2019 International Results in Mathematics and Science*. Boston, MA: TIMSS and PIRLS International Study Center. https://timssandpirls.bc.edu/timss2019/international-results/.

Mullis, Ina V. S., Michael O. Martin, Chad A. Minnich, Kathleen T. Drucker, and Moira A. Ragan. 2012. *PIRLS 2011 Encyclopedia: Education Policy and Curriculum in Reading, Volumes 1 and 2*. Chestnut Hill, MA: TIMSS and PIRLS International Study Center, Lynch School of Education, Boston College.

OECD (Organisation for Economic Co-operation and Development). 2018. *PISA for Development Assessment and Analytical Framework: Reading, Mathematics and Science*. Paris, France: OECD Publishing. https://doi.org/10.1787/9789264305274-en.

OECD (Organisation for Economic Co-operation and Development). 2019. *PISA 2018 Results, Volume I: What Students Know and Can Do*. Paris: OECD Publishing. https://doi.org/10.1787/5f07c754-en.

International Assessment Organization Websites

PISA: https://www.oecd.org/pisa

TIMSS and PIRLS: https://timssandpirls.bc.edu

International Association for the Evaluation of Educational Achievement publications on Reliability and Validity of International Large-Scale Assessment: https://www.iea.nl/index.php/publications/series-journals/iea-research-education/reliability-and-validity-international-large

Chapter 9 WHAT ARE THE MAIN REGIONAL LARGE-SCALE STUDENT ASSESSMENTS?

Regional large-scale assessments are an alternative for countries interested in comparing their achievement levels with those of geographically proximate or linguistically similar countries. They can be a useful addition or alternative to participation in the international large-scale assessments discussed in chapter 8. This chapter discusses five of these regional large-scale assessments. Table 8A.1 compares each assessment on key dimensions. Additional information can be found by visiting the official websites or contacting the sponsoring organization for each assessment (see the reference section of this chapter).

Southern and Eastern Africa Consortium for Monitoring Educational Quality

The Southern and Eastern Africa Consortium for Monitoring Educational Quality (SACMEQ) was launched in 1995 with the support of the International Institute for Educational Planning of the United Nations Educational, Scientific, and Cultural Organization (UNESCO) and the government of the Netherlands. The consortium includes ministries of education in southern and eastern Africa, including Botswana, Eswatini, Kenya, Lesotho, Malawi, Mauritius, Mozambique, Namibia, Seychelles, South Africa, Tanzania (mainland and Zanzibar), Uganda, Zambia, and Zimbabwe (Hungi et al. 2010).

SACMEQ promotes collaboration among its members, who share experiences and expertise in building the capacity of education planners to evaluate educational quality using scientific methods. The consortium facilitates technical training focused on skills required for monitoring and evaluation, designing effective reports, and strategies for dissemination to ensure that stakeholders and decision makers for policy reform widely discuss and understand results (Hungi et al. 2010).

The SACMEQ assessments are administered to grade 6 students attending public or independent mainstream schools in participating countries. There have been four rounds of SACMEQ studies—the first from 1995 to 1999, the second from 2000 to 2004, the third from 2006 to 2011, and the fourth from 2012 to 2014. Table 9.1 lists the countries that participated in each SACMEQ round. Consistent with the previous study rounds, the fourth round (SACMEQ IV) measured student knowledge and skills in reading and mathematics. Although overall results are not available for SACMEQ IV, there are some reports on individual country performance (SACMEQ 2017). More extensive findings are available for SACMEQ III.

The SACMEQ reading assessment has eight competency levels (table 9.2). The lowest level, prereading, measures the ability to match words and pictures; the highest level, critical reading, measures the ability to infer and evaluate a writer's assumptions in different parts of a text.

The SACMEQ mathematics assessment also has eight competency levels (table 9.3). Prenumeracy knowledge and skills is the lowest competency level measured; students performing at this level can perform single-step addition and subtraction operations. The highest competency level measures the ability to solve mathematical problems and tasks embedded in verbal or graphic information (SACMEQ 2017).

SACMEQ includes contextual questionnaires for students that ask about factors believed to influence teaching and learning in schools. There are also questionnaires for teachers and school principals (SACMEQ 2017).

SACMEQ results are reported as scaled scores, percentages, and competency levels. SACMEQ III collected data from approximately 61,000 students; 8,000 teachers; and 2,800 school principals; average reading and mathematics scores are shown in table 9.4. The average score on the SACMEQ scale is 500 points; countries with average scores above this value are described as having "above

TABLE 9.1. Countries That Have Participated in Each Round of the Southern and Eastern Africa Consortium for Monitoring Educational Quality

Round	Countries
I	Kenya, Malawi, Mauritius, Namibia, Zambia, Zanzibar, Zimbabwe
II	Botswana, Eswatini, Kenya, Lesotho, Malawi, Mauritius, Mozambique, Namibia, Seychelles, South Africa, Tanzania (mainland and Zanzibar), Uganda, Zambia
III	Botswana, Kenya, Lesotho, Malawi, Mauritius, Namibia, Seychelles, South Africa, Tanzania (mainland and Zanzibar), Zambia, Zimbabwe
IV	Botswana, Eswatini, Kenya, Lesotho, Malawi, Mauritius, Mozambique, Namibia, Seychelles, South Africa, Tanzania (mainland and Zanzibar), Uganda, Zambia, Zimbabwe

Source: Original compilation for this publication.

Note: Results for the fourth round are publicly available only for Botswana, Mauritius, Namibia, and South Africa.

TABLE 9.2. Southern and Eastern Africa Consortium for Monitoring Educational Quality Reading Competency Levels and Descriptors

	Level	Descriptor	Competencies
Basic reading skills	1	Prereading	Matches words and pictures involving concrete concepts and everyday objects
	2	Emergent reading	Matches words and pictures involving prepositions and abstract concepts
	3	Basic reading	Interprets meaning by matching words and phrases, completing sentences
	4	Reading for meaning	Reads to link and interpret information located in various parts of the text
	5	Interpretive reading	Interprets information from various parts of the text in association with external information
Advanced reading skills	6	Inferential reading	Reads to combine information from various parts of the text to infer the writer's purpose
	7	Analytical reading	Locates and combines information from various parts of the text to infer the writer's personal beliefs
	8	Critical reading	Reads from various parts of the text to infer and evaluate what the writer has assumed about the topic and the characteristics of the reader

Source: Adapted from SACMEQ 2017.

TABLE 9.3. Southern and Eastern Africa Consortium for Monitoring Educational Quality Mathematics Competency Levels and Descriptors

	Level	Descriptor	Competencies
Basic math skills	1	Prenumeracy	Applies single-step addition and subtraction
	2	Emergent numeracy	Applies two-step addition and subtraction involving carrying
	3	Basic numeracy	Translates verbal information into arithmetic operations
	4	Beginning numeracy	Translates verbal or graphic information into simple arithmetic problems
	5	Competent numeracy	Translates verbal, graphic, or tabular information into an arithmetic form to solve a problem
Advanced math skills	6	Mathematically skilled	Solves multiple-operation problems (using the correct order) involving fractions, ratios, and decimals
	7	Concrete problem solving	Extracts and converts information from tables, charts, and other symbolic presentations to identify and solve multistep problems
	8	Abstract problem solving	Identifies the nature of an unstated mathematical problem embedded in verbal or graphic information and translates this information into symbolic, algebraic, or equation form to solve a problem

Source: Adapted from SACMEQ 2017.

TABLE 9.4. Southern and Eastern Africa Consortium for Monitoring Educational Quality Third Round Reading and Mathematics Average Scores, According to Country

Region	Reading	Mathematics
	Mean (standard error)	
Botswana	534.6 (4.57)	520.5 (3.51)
Eswatini	549.4 (2.98)	540.8 (2.39)
Kenya	543.1 (4.92)	557.0 (3.98)
Lesotho	467.9 (2.86)	476.9 (2.61)
Malawi	433.5 (2.63)	447.0 (2.89)
Mauritius	573.5 (4.92)	623.3 (5.83)
Mozambique	476.0 (2.82)	483.8 (2.29)
Namibia	496.9 (2.99)	471.0 (2.51)
Seychelles	575.1 (3.10)	550.7 (2.45)
South Africa	494.9 (4.55)	494.8 (3.81)
Tanzania (mainland)	577.8 (3.40)	552.7 (3.51)
Tanzania-Zanzibar	536.8 (3.11)	489.9 (2.35)
Uganda	478.7 (3.46)	481.9 (2.92)
Zambia	434.4 (3.37)	435.2 (2.45)
Zimbabwe	507.7 (5.65)	519.8 (4.98)

Source: Adapted from Hungi et al. 2010.

average" performance on the assessment. Tanzania (mainland), Seychelles, and Mauritius had the highest average performance in reading; Mauritius, Kenya, and Tanzania (mainland) had the highest average achievement in mathematics (Hungi et al. 2010).

Tailored reports for SACMEQ III were produced for each participating country, highlighting things of particular importance for that country. For instance, Namibia's SACMEQ III report highlighted that 73 percent of tested grade 6 students had at least one exercise book, pencil or pen, and ruler as part of their basic materials for working at school but that only 32 percent reported having their own mathematics textbook, which was below the average (41 percent) for participating countries (Amadila et al. 2011).

SACMEQ studies have supported a diverse range of policy objectives in participating countries, including monitoring levels and trends in reading and mathematics achievement, knowledge of HIV-AIDS prevention and HIV-AIDS education programs, gender equality and gender gaps in reading and mathematics, trends in grade repetition, equity in provision of human and material resources among regions and schools, and gender equality in school managerial positions (SACMEQ 2017).

Programme d'Analyse des Systèmes Éducatifs de la CONFEMEN

The Programme d'Analyse des Systèmes Éducatifs de la CONFEMEN (PASEC) is an assessment program of the Conférence des Ministres de l'Éducation des Etats et Gouvernements de la Francophonie (CONFEMEN). It is mainly administered to students in francophone countries in West and Central Africa and Madagascar; it has also been implemented in Cambodia, China, Laos, Lebanon, and Vietnam (PASEC 2015).

PASEC has three main objectives: produce robust, reliable data on learning; use assessment results for educational reform; and increase national assessment capacities in participating countries. PASEC is administered to students in grades 2 and 6. The results are used to understand the effectiveness and equity of primary education in participating countries while also considering the school and extracurricular factors that affect student learning (PASEC 2015).

PASEC was introduced in 1991, and 24 francophone countries participated on a rolling basis between 1991 and 2010. In 2012, the assessment underwent extensive reforms to improve its methodology. A new version was implemented in Benin, Burkina Faso, Burundi, Cameroon, Chad, the Democratic Republic of Congo, Côte d'Ivoire, Niger, Senegal, and Togo in 2013/14. The next PASEC assessment was administered in 2019, with Benin, Burkina Faso, Burundi, Cameroon, Chad, the Democratic Republic of Congo, the Republic of Congo, Côte d'Ivoire, Gabon, Guinea, Madagascar, Mali, Niger, Senegal, and Togo participating. The results for the 2019 assessment have yet to be released.

The most recent PASEC assessment for which results are available (2014) was developed and administered in the official language of instruction for most participating countries (French). Translations and context adaptations allowed for administration of the assessment in English in Cameroon and in Kirundi in Burundi (PASEC 2015).

In contrast with other regional and international learning assessments, which are typically administered at the end of the school year, PASEC 2014 was implemented at the beginning of the school year to help diagnose student abilities in the language of instruction and mathematics and identify common barriers that students encounter in the learning process so that they can be addressed before these barriers limit student achievement, possibly leading to failure or dropping out of school (PASEC 2015).

Box 9.1 summarizes the content that the 2014 PASEC assessments covered (PASEC 2015). Although grade 2 and 6 assessments for each subject area cover similar topics, they differ in the complexity and cognitive demand of their assessment tasks. For instance, the reading comprehension tasks in grade 2 involve decoding the meaning of words and understanding sentences and short texts; the equivalent tasks in grade 6 involve comprehending and inferring information from longer literary and informational texts. PASEC 2014 also included background questionnaires for students, teachers, head teachers, and ministers of education.

BOX 9.1. Areas Assessed in Programme d'Analyse des Systèmes Éducatifs de la CONFEMEN 2014

Grade 2. Language of instruction assessment

Listening comprehension: Assessed using oral messages consisting of isolated words, sentences, and passages.

Familiarization with written language and reading decoding: Assessed using exercises requiring that students recognize characteristics of the written language, grapho-phonological identification, and simple letter and word reading activities.

Reading comprehension: Assessed using exercises requiring that students read isolated words and sentences as well as texts and then find, combine, and interpret information. Developing competencies in this area enables students to read autonomously in a variety of day-to-day situations and thereby develop knowledge and participate in society.

Grade 2. Mathematics assessment

Arithmetic: Assessed using exercises requiring pupils to count, quantify, and handle quantities of objects, perform operations, complete series of numbers, and solve problems.

Geometry, space, and measurement: Assessed according to recognition of geometric shapes and the concepts of size and orientation in space.

Grade 6. Language-of-instruction assessment

Decoding isolated words and sentences: Assessed according to grapho-phonological recognition of words and ability to decode the meaning of isolated words and sentences.

Reading comprehension: Assessed using exercises that require students to read literary and informative texts and other documents; extract, combine, and interpret one or several pieces of information; and make simple inferences.

Grade 6. Mathematics assessment

Arithmetic: Assessed using exercises requiring that students recognize, apply, and solve problems using operations, whole numbers, decimal numbers, fractions, percentages, series of numbers, and data tables.

Measurement: Assessed using exercises requiring that students recognize, apply, and solve problems involving the concept of size: length, mass, capacity, surface area, and perimeter.

Geometry and space: Assessed according to recognition of the properties of two- and three-dimensional geometric shapes, geometric relationships and transformations, and orientation in and visualization of space.

Source: Adapted from PASEC 2015.

PASEC 2014 results are reported on a common scale with an average of 500. Findings from the 2014 grade 2 assessments revealed that students from Burundi, on average, scored higher than their peers on the language and mathematics assessments (figure 9.1). Other high-scoring countries were the Republic of Congo, Burkina Faso, and Senegal.

Information on percentages of students in participating countries that achieve different competency benchmarks complements these average scores. For example, on the grade 2 language assessment, PASEC 2014 defines five competency levels—below early reader, early reader, emerging reader, novice reader, intermediate reader—and one competency threshold (sufficient). Table 9.5 summarizes the percentage of grade 2 students who achieved each of these competency levels in 2014; fewer than 30 percent of students achieved sufficient language competency, which is linked to ability to decode written language and understand sentences, passages, and oral messages.

FIGURE 9.1. **Average Grade 2 Programme d'Analyse des Systèmes Éducatifs de la CONFEMEN 2014 Scores in Language and Mathematics**

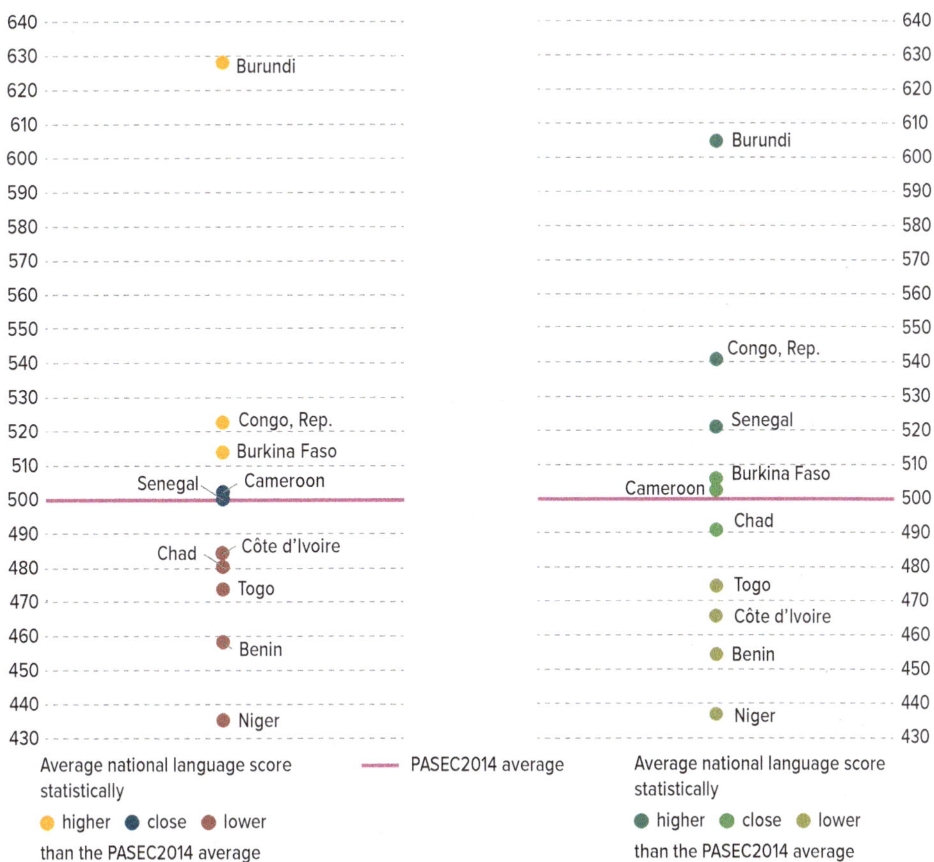

Source: PASEC 2015.

TABLE 9.5. Programme d'Analyse des Systèmes Éducatifs de la CONFEMEN 2014: Language of Instruction Competency Scale for Grade 2

Level	Minimum score	Percentage of students	Description
4	610.4	14.1	Intermediate reader: enhanced reading autonomy bolsters student understanding of sentences and texts. Students have acquired written language decoding and listening comprehension competencies.
3	540.0	14.5	Novice reader: gradual improvement in written language decoding, listening comprehension, and reading comprehension skills. Able to understand meaning of heard or read words.
Sufficient competency threshold			
2	469.5	28.7	Emerging reader: gradual development of written language decoding skills and reinforcement of listening comprehension skills. Able to make basic links between oral and written language.
1	399.1	30.3	Early reader: first contact with oral and written language. Able to understand very short, familiar oral messages.
Below 1	126.0	12.4	Pupils at this level do not display the competencies measured by this assessment.

Source: Adapted from PASEC 2015.

Laboratorio Latinoamericano de Evaluación de la Calidad de la Educación

The Laboratorio Latinoamericano de Evaluación de la Calidad de la Educación (LLECE) was founded in 1994 as the network of National Systems for Measurement and Evaluation of Educational Quality in Latin America to oversee the development of comparative studies on educational quality in Latin America (Flotts et al. 2016). It is coordinated by UNESCO's Oficina Regional de Educación para América Latina y el Caribe (OREALC).

LLECE's objective is to assess student learning in the core knowledge domains of language, mathematics, and science. OREALC uses the results from these assessments to inform educational policies, support capacity building for development of assessment systems, and promote exchange of ideas among countries. The fact that a commensurate increase in learning has not accompanied a large increase in school enrollment rates in Latin American countries over the past decades supports the importance of OREALC's continued focus on improving educational quality (Flotts et al. 2016).

There have been four LLECE assessment rounds. The first was administered in 1997 and focused on reading and mathematics in grades 3 and 4. The second was administered in 2006 and measured reading and mathematics in grades 3 and 6 and science in grade 6. The third was conducted in 2013 and targeted the same grades and subjects as the second (Flotts et al. 2016). The results of the fourth, administered in 2019 and also covering the same grades and subjects as the second, will be released in 2021. Table 9.6 lists the countries that participated in each LLECE assessment study round.

The assessment framework and test blueprints for the third study round, developed based on a review of common content of the national curricula of participating countries, led OREALC to include curriculum features in the assessment framework specific to the region and not reflected in other international large-scale assessments (Flotts et al. 2016; Greaney and Kellaghan 2008).

Boxes 9.2 to 9.4 describe the content domains and cognitive processes assessed in the reading, mathematics, and science assessments used for the

TABLE 9.6. Country Participation in Laboratorio Latinoamericano de Evaluación de la Calidad de la Educación Studies

Round	Countries
First	Argentina; Bolivia; Brazil; Chile; Colombia; Costa Rica; Cuba; Dominican Republic; Honduras; Mexico; Paraguay; Peru; Venezuela, RB
Second	Argentina, Brazil, Chile, Colombia, Costa Rica, Cuba, Dominican Republic, Ecuador, El Salvador, Guatemala, Mexico, Nicaragua, Panama, Paraguay, Peru, Uruguay
Third	Argentina, Brazil, Chile, Colombia, Costa Rica, Dominican Republic, Ecuador, Guatemala, Honduras, Mexico, Nicaragua, Panama, Paraguay, Peru, Uruguay
Fourth	Argentina, Bolivia, Brazil, Chile, Colombia, Costa Rica, Cuba, Dominican Republic, Ecuador, El Salvador, Guatemala, Honduras, Mexico, Nicaragua, Panama, Paraguay, Peru, Uruguay

Source: Original compilation for this publication.

BOX 9.2. Content Domains and Cognitive Processes Assessed in the Third Laboratorio Latinoamericano de Evaluación de la Calidad de la Educación Reading Assessment

Content domains

Text comprehension: reading of continuous and discontinuous texts, from which an intra- or inter-textual task is performed

Metalinguistic and theoretical: mastery of language and literature concepts, which focus on language through knowledge of concepts and recognition of text characteristics

Cognitive processes

Literal understanding: skills linked to identification of explicit elements of a text and location of information in specific segments of a text

Inferential understanding: skills related to integrating pieces of information included in different sections of a text to understand its main purpose and skills linked to splitting complex information into its more basic elements and establishing relationships between these basic pieces of information

Critical understanding: skills linked to assessing the text author's point of view and distinguishing it from or contrasting it with others' point of view

Source: Adapted from Flotts et al. 2016.

BOX 9.3. Content Domains and Cognitive Processes Assessed in the Third Laboratorio Latinoamericano de Evaluación de la Calidad de la Educación Mathematics Assessment

Content domains

Numerical domain: number meaning and number system structure, representation and construction of numerical relationships, appropriate use of operations to solve problems (addition, subtraction, multiplication, division, and exponentials)

Geometric domain: properties of two- and three-dimensional objects; translation, displacement, and rotation of geometric shapes; similarity of geometric shapes; and construction of geometric shapes

Measurement domain: magnitudes and estimates; uses of measurement units, patterns, and currencies

Statistical domain: use and interpretation of data and information, measures of central tendency, and data representations

Variation domain: numerical and geometric patterns, variable identification, notions of function, and direct and inverse proportionality

Cognitive processes

Recognition of objects and elements: identification of facts, relationships, properties, and mathematical concepts expressed directly and explicitly in a statement

Solving simple problems: use of mathematical information referring to a single variable expressed explicitly in a statement to reach the solution

Solution of complex problems: reorganization of mathematical information presented in a statement and structuring of a solution based on nonexplicit relationships involving more than one variable

Source: Adapted from Flotts et al. 2016.

BOX 9.4. Content Domains and Cognitive Processes Assessed in the Third Laboratorio Latinoamericano de Evaluación de la Calidad de la Educación Science Assessment

Content domains

Health: knowledge of structure and functioning of human body

Life: identification of organisms and their characteristics, classification of living beings

Environment: interaction between organisms and their environment

Earth and solar system: physical characteristics of Earth, movements of Earth and moon and their relationship with observable natural phenomena, atmosphere, and some climatic phenomena

Matter and energy: elementary notions about properties of matter (weight, volume, temperature), and forms of energy

Source: Adapted from Flotts et al. 2016.

third round. The same domains and cognitive processes are measured in the grades 3 and 6 assessments for each subject area but with greater emphasis on complex tasks in the higher grade. For instance, the grade 6 reading assessment includes a higher proportion of items focused on measuring critical understanding of texts. Similarly, the grade 6 mathematics assessment includes more items that require students to produce solutions to complex problems in which the mathematical relationship between variables is not explicit (Flotts et al. 2016).

Background questionnaires were administered to students, families, teachers, and school principals. Student questionnaires were used to gather information about demographic characteristics, availability of educational materials in school and at home, relationships with peers and teachers, and extracurricular activities. Parent questionnaires asked about family and neighborhood characteristics, availability of educational materials at home, attitude to reading, student behavior, and school-related support at home. Teacher questionnaires inquired about their demographic characteristics, teaching experience, work environment, and school management. School principal questionnaires asked about school infrastructure, materials, and school management (Flotts et al. 2016).

Table 9.7 presents average grade 3 reading and mathematics scores for countries participating in the third Laboratorio Latinoamericano de Evaluación de

TABLE 9.7. Mean Grade 3 Reading and Mathematics Scores on the Third Laboratorio Latinoamericano de Evaluación de la Calidad de la Educación Study

Country	Reading	Mathematics
	Mean (Standard Error)	
Argentina	703 (4.89)	717 (4.83)
Brazil	712 (4.99)	727 (6.05)
Chile	802 (3.96)	787 (4.04)
Colombia	714 (8.33)	694 (7.80)
Costa Rica	754 (3.24)	750 (2.86)
Dominican Republic	614 (3.50)	602 (3.68)
Ecuador	698 (4.72)	703 (4.75)
Guatemala	678 (3.87)	672 (3.28)
Honduras	681 (4.14)	680 (4.97)
Mexico	718 (3.25)	741 (3.26)
Nicaragua	654 (2.84)	653 (3.07)
Panama	670 (3.94)	664 (4.45)
Paraguay	653 (4.81)	652 (5.42)
Peru	719 (3.91)	716 (4.10)
Uruguay	728 (7.15)	742 (7.96)

Source: Adapted from Flotts et al. 2016.

la Calidad de la Educación study. The scale mean is 700. Chile, Costa Rica, and Uruguay had the highest average scores on both assessments.

Results were also reported according to proficiency level and showed that 39 percent of students in grade 3 reached the two highest proficiency levels on the reading assessment. These students can comprehend, establish relationships between concepts, and interpret and infer meaning in complex texts about unfamiliar topics; 29 percent of students in grade 3 were able to achieve the two highest proficiency levels in mathematics, demonstrating their capacity to solve complex mathematical problems that involve arithmetic operations, geometry, and interpretation of information based on tables and plots (Flotts et al. 2016).

Pacific Islands Literacy and Numeracy Assessment

The Educational Quality and Assessment Programme (EQAP) of the Pacific Community oversees design and implementation of the Pacific Islands Literacy and Numeracy Assessment (PILNA), which measures numeracy and literacy skills of students who have completed grades 4 and 6 (SPC and EQAP 2019).

The main objective of PILNA is to monitor and improve learning outcomes of students in the Pacific Island countries using a shared framework and to explore the cognitive and contextual factors that facilitate student achievement in the region. EQAP and supporting partners also aim to build capacity for assessment development and strengthen learning assessment and educational standards and policies through engagement and collaboration with participating countries (SPC and EQAP 2019).

There have been three PILNA studies—the first completed in 2012, the second in 2015, and the third in 2018 (SPC and EQAP 2019). Table 9.8 lists the countries that participated in each PILNA assessment round.

PILNA's assessment framework was developed based on shared regional learning standards. EQAP and country representatives reviewed the national curricula of participating countries and identified the common curriculum components and learning outcomes for incorporation into PILNA's framework and definition of regional benchmarks (SPC and EQAP 2019).

PILNA measures the foundational knowledge, understanding, and skills that are necessary to participate effectively in society. The assessment framework defines literacy as "The knowledge and skills necessary to empower a person to

TABLE 9.8. Country Participation in Pacific Islands Literacy and Numeracy Assessment Studies

Study	Countries
First	Cook Islands, Federal States of Micronesia, Fiji, Kiribati, Marshall Islands, Nauru, Niue, Palau, Papua New Guinea, Samoa, Solomon Islands, Tokelau, Tonga, Tuvalu
Second	Cook Islands, Federal States of Micronesia, Kiribati, Marshall Islands, Niue, Palau, Papua New Guinea, Samoa, Solomon Islands, Tokelau, Tonga, Tuvalu
Third	Cook Islands, Federal States of Micronesia, Fiji, Kiribati, Marshall Islands, Nauru, Niue, Palau, Papua New Guinea, Samoa, Solomon Islands, Tokelau, Tonga, Tuvalu

Source: Original compilation for this publication.

communicate through any form of language in their society and the wider world, with respect to all aspects of everyday life" (SPC and EQAP 2019, p. 1). Table 9.9 presents the benchmark indicators for the four PILNA literacy domains: reading, writing, listening, and speaking.

PILNA's definition of numeracy is, "The knowledge and skills necessary to empower a person to be able to use mathematical processes, as well as the language of mathematics, for a variety of purposes, with respect to everyday life" (SPC and EQAP 2019, p. 1). Table 9.10 summarizes benchmark indicators for the five numeracy assessment domains: numbers, operations, measurement and geometry, and data.

PILNA defines nine proficiency levels for literacy and numeracy; results are also expressed and reported as scaled scores, with a mean of 500 and a standard deviation of 50. Students performing at the lowest level on the numeracy assessment are not able to write a two-digit number or complete increasing patterns defined by a simple relationship. Students performing at the highest proficiency level can solve complex word problems involving mixed operations, convert metric lengths into different measurement units, and calculate the probability of events (SPC and EQAP 2019).

Figure 9.2 shows the proportion of grade 4 students in each of the numeracy proficiency levels defined for PILNA. Results are disaggregated according to study cycle. They show an upward trend in the proportion of students reaching the highest levels of proficiency over time, indicating improvements in education in the Pacific Island nations that have resulted in greater numeracy achievement in grade 4.

PILNA 2018 results suggest a positive correlation between school resources and student achievement in numeracy and literacy (table 9.11). To determine

TABLE 9.9. Pacific Islands Literacy and Numeracy Assessment 2018 Literacy Benchmarks for Grades 4 and 6

Domain	Grade 4	Grade 6
Reading	Understand and engage with a variety of texts with some complexity of ideas and a less predictable structure	Use comprehension strategies to interpret and evaluate a variety of texts of increasing complexity in content and structure
Writing	Present ideas and information using mostly simple sentences and paragraphs to create a range of texts	Use a variety of writing conventions to present ideas and information on a wide range of topics and text types
Listening	Use listening strategies to understand and respond to aural or spoken texts of some complexity from a variety of settings, experiences, and learning contexts	Use listening strategies to understand, evaluate, and respond to a wide variety of aural and spoken texts of increasing complexity in content and structure
Speaking	Use language structures of some complexity to convey ideas and experiences in a variety of contexts	Use complex language structures to communicate ideas and experiences in a variety of contexts effectively

Source: Adapted from SPC and EQAP 2019.

TABLE 9.10. Pacific Islands Literacy and Numeracy Assessment 2018 Numeracy Benchmarks for Grades 4 and 6

Domain	Grade 4	Grade 6
Numbers	• Recognize, represent, and compare quantities • Use place value to show understanding of the number system • Interpret number sequences using simple rules to solve problems • Understand equivalence of fractions	• Demonstrate understanding of numbers and their magnitude, properties, and relationships • Interpret relationships and properties of number sequences and fractions expressed in different forms
Operations	• Use various representations and demonstrate mathematical skills to solve problems involving arithmetic operations	• Demonstrate mathematical skills in linking various arithmetic operations to solve problems set in a range of familiar situations
Measurement and geometry	• Develop awareness of different measurable quantities, units of measure and conversion between them, and measurement tools • Show spatial and geometric skills by measuring and calculating with physical attributes of common objects and events and by comparing and working with properties of shapes and figures	• Develop and use patterns and rules to facilitate calculation with measurable quantities • Work with properties of geometric figures and objects
Data	• Collect, organize, represent, and interpret data in various ways	• Collect and represent data in tables and graphs • Interpret and analyze results • Recognize and use mathematical language related to common and familiar chance events

Source: Adapted from SPC and EQAP 2019.

FIGURE 9.2. Proportion of Students in Each Numeracy Proficiency Level in Grade 4: Pacific Islands Literacy and Numeracy Assessment, 2012–18

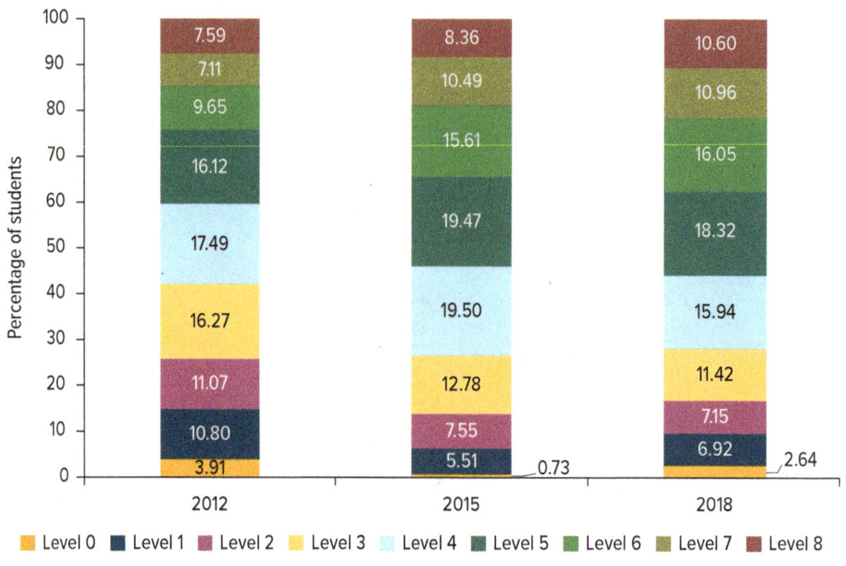

Source: SPC and EQAP 2019.

TABLE 9.11. Association between School Resources and Student Achievement

Subject	Correlation (Standard Error)
Numeracy	
Grade 4	0.05 (0.02)
Grade 6	0.07 (0.02)
Literacy	
Grade 4	0.12 (0.03)
Grade 6	0.13 (0.03)

Source: SPC and EQAP 2019.

Note: All correlations were statistically significant (*p-value*<0.05).

the association between these school-level factors and student achievement, the PILNA team calculated a school-level resource measure for each participating school, based on availability of specific resources (for example, photocopy machines, school library, internet access, computers for teachers and students, and a sick room). The positive correlations suggest the importance of providing adequate resources to schools to foster student learning.

Southeast Asia Primary Learning Metrics

The Southeast Asian Ministers of Education Organization (SEAMEO) developed the Southeast Asia Primary Learning Metrics (SEA-PLM) assessment, the most recent of the regional assessments, in collaboration with the United Nations Children's Fund (UNICEF). Similar to PILNA, the assessment team behind SEA-PLM received capacity-building and technical support from international assessment organizations (UNICEF and SEAMEO 2017a).

The main goal of the SEA-PLM exercise is to monitor system-level student learning to improve education quality in participating SEAMEO countries. The SEA-PLM exercise is designed to provide meaningful information to policy makers about the quality of their education systems and greater understanding of the factors that affect student learning. It assesses student knowledge, skills, and understanding in four domains (mathematical literacy, reading literacy, writing literacy, global citizenship) and is designed to increase the assessment capacity of participating countries (UNICEF and SEAMEO 2017a).

The assessment development process started in 2015 with development of the assessment framework and item writing activities, including translation and piloting of items in participating countries. In 2018, the SEA-PLM team finalized the sampling framework for data collection, and in 2019, SEA-PLM was administered to a representative population of grade 5 students in six Southeast Asian countries: Cambodia, Lao People's Democratic Republic, Malaysia, Myanmar, Philippines, and Vietnam. Reports and dissemination activities are scheduled for 2020 and 2021 (UNICEF and SEAMEO 2017a).

For three of the four domains assessed (mathematical literacy, reading literacy, writing literacy), the assessment frameworks were developed after in-depth review and analysis of participating countries' curricula and other sources of information. The assessment team reviewed grade-wise curricula and learning standards in these areas, descriptions of national assessment programs and classroom assessment guidelines, time allocations for each subject, and descriptions of transitions from mother tongue to official language of instruction in some countries. Common curricular elements identified during the review were used to develop the final SEA-PLM frameworks for mathematics, reading, and writing (UNICEF and SEAMEO 2017a).

For the SEA-PLM 2019 exercise, the mathematical literacy domain was defined as a "person's capacity, given a problem in a context that is of interest or importance to them, to translate the problem into a suitable mathematical formulation, to apply mathematical knowledge and skills to find a solution, and to interpret the mathematical results in relation to the context and to review the merits or limitations of those results" (UNICEF and SEAMEO 2017a, p. 15).

The mathematical literacy domain comprises several subdomains, including numeric and algebraic literacy, measurement and geometry, and probability and data analysis. Each subdomain features items that require cognitive processing of mathematical information at different levels of complexity to arrive at a solution (box 9.5). In many of the tasks included in the mathematical literacy assessment, understanding and expressing a stimulus using mathematical terms is required, rather than producing numerical calculations. Real-life problems included on the SEA-PLM 2019 assessment are not limited to a specific subdomain but rather require students to combine aspects of different content areas to reach a solution (UNICEF and SEAMEO 2017a).

The reading literacy domain is defined as "understanding, using and responding to a range of written texts, in order to meet personal, societal, economic and civic needs" (UNICEF and SEAMEO 2017a, p. 23). This definition highlights the relevance of literacy as a process that involves, but goes beyond, decoding to include location and interpretation of information, understanding the purpose of a text, and using text information to evaluate knowledge of the world (UNICEF and SEAMEO 2017a).

BOX 9.5. Cognitive Processes Assessed in the Southeast Asia Primary Learning Metrics 2019 Mathematical Literacy Assessment

Cognitive processes

Translate: expressing a problem in mathematical language—taking it from the context to a mathematical formulation suitable for finding a solution

Apply: using mathematical knowledge and skills to find a mathematical solution or to generate mathematical results; mainly using mathematical ideas, objects, and techniques

Interpret and review: translating mathematical solutions to the context of the problem

Source: Adapted from UNICEF and SEAMEO 2017a.

Content subdomains of the reading literacy assessment comprise items that measure proficiency with particular text types and formats. Text format refers to the way in which a text is organized (continuous, discontinuous, or composite). Continuous texts are structured in sentences and paragraphs; discontinuous texts include information arranged in diagrams, tables, maps, or lists; and composite texts include information arranged in continuous and discontinuous formats, such as opinion pieces or pages in newspapers (UNICEF and SEAMEO 2017a). Box 9.6 summarizes the text types and cognitive processes included in SEA-PLM.

SEA-PLM defines writing literacy as "constructing meaning by generating a range of written texts to express oneself and communicate with others, in order to meet personal, societal, economic and civic needs." (UNICEF and SEAMEO 2017a, p. 32). This definition emphasizes the capacity to form words but also involves spelling correctly, constructing meaning in written messages, and having a specific purpose for the message (UNICEF and SEAMEO 2017a).

Content subdomains within the writing assessment comprise items that target student proficiency with narrative, descriptive, persuasive, instructional, and transactional writing tasks. Although the definition of each writing type is similar to the list of text types described in box 9.6, the items present a task and require the student to write an answer. Because the answer depends on a student's writing capacity, each item is scored using a marking guide that allows for partial credit (UNICEF and SEAMEO 2017a).

For the global citizenship assessment, the assessment team conducted a systematic review of global citizenship education and identified a set of core regional values as defined in the documents obtained from the Association of Southeast Asian Nations. These sources informed the definition of the global citizenship domain and the identification of global citizenship outcomes that could be included as part of the assessment (UNICEF and SEAMEO 2017b).

SEA-PLM 2019 defines global citizens as individuals who "appreciate and understand the interconnectedness of all life on the planet. They act and relate to others with this understanding to make the world a more peaceful, just, safe, and sustainable place" (UNICEF and SEAMEO 2017b, p. 7). The assessment framework indicates that the key concept in this definition is *interconnectedness*, the idea that local actions might have global consequences and, conversely, that global events can have local effects on peace, equity, safety, and sustainability (UNICEF and SEAMEO 2017b).

The global citizenship domain includes three subdomains: systems, issues, and dynamics; awareness and identities; and engagement. Global citizenship systems are systems that reflect and support the interconnectedness of life on the planet and the multilevel dynamics that affect students' lived experiences and the global distribution of wealth, power, and environmental sustainability. The global citizenship awareness and identities subdomain explores individuals' multiple identities and how these identities relate to their roles as global citizens; this subdomain emphasizes respect and acceptance of diversity within and between communities. Global citizenship engagement is linked to the ways in

BOX 9.6. The Text Types and Cognitive Processes Assessed in the Southeast Asia Primary Learning Metrics 2019 Reading Literacy Assessment

Text types

Narrative: present and develop characters, events, and themes and answer questions relating to "when" or "in what sequence"

Descriptive: present information about people or objects and abstract concepts and address "what" and some "how" types of questions

Persuasive: represent points of view used to persuade the reader in texts that address some "which" and "why" questions

Instructional: explain how to complete a specified task and address some "how" and "when" questions

Transactional: achieve a specific purpose involving an exchange of information between two or more parties

Label: identify something using text consisting of a single word, or a small set of words; categorize images or words presented in isolation to assess some of the precursor skills of reading

Cognitive processes

Word recognition: recognize written form of a word with its meaning

Locate: locate specific or general information in a text

Interpret: understand ideas not directly stated in a text by identifying relationships between ideas, understanding assumptions, synthesizing different pieces of information, or identifying the main idea in a text

Reflect: link information in the text with wider knowledge based on the reader's experience (for example, identify intended audience of a text or the attitude of the author, evaluate arguments)

Source: Adapted from UNICEF and SEAMEO 2017a.

which students can contribute as global citizens. Box 9.7 presents examples of each subdomain (UNICEF and SEAMEO 2017b).

The first set of results for SEA-PLM were released in 2020. They will provide policy makers, stakeholders, and international organizations with valuable comparative information on achievement levels in some countries that have never participated in regional or international learning assessments, for example, Myanmar.

SEA-PLM reading, writing, and mathematics results are expressed in proficiency levels (referred to as "bands") that describe what students know and can do. Students reaching the highest proficiency level have mastered the fundamental skills expected of them by the end of primary school, including twenty-first century skills such as communication, use of technology, and critical thinking (UNICEF and SEAMEO 2020).

BOX 9.7. Examples of Global Citizenship Subdomains Measured in the Southeast Asia Primary Learning Metrics 2019 Assessment

Systems, issues, and dynamics

- Organization of societies and the world
- Changes of rules, laws, and responsibilities over time and their dynamics
- Common basic needs and rights
- Global injustice
- Values and skills that enable people to live together peacefully
- Environmental sustainability, such as global warming and climate change
- Relationships between local and global issues

Awareness and identities

- The self, family, school, neighborhood, community, country, and the world
- Similarities and differences between people, societies, and cultures
- Diversity in society
- Connections and relationships among communities
- Factors that influence people's attitudes and values

Engagement

- Individuals and groups taking positive action to improve the community without harming others
- Roles played by voluntary groups, social movements, and citizens in improving their communities and identifying solutions to global problems
- Benefits and consequences of personal and collective civic engagement
- Public dialogue and debate
- Sustainable consumption habits

Source: Adapted from UNICEF and SEAMEO (2017b).

Figure 9.3 presents the SEA-PLM results for reading. Students reaching proficiency level 6 or above can read with comprehension, use explicit and implicit information from various text types with familiar structures, and compare multiple pieces of information to produce new ideas. Students below proficiency level 2 can find the meaning of some words in a text but cannot read a range of everyday texts fluently and engage with their meaning. The majority of students assessed in Malaysia and Vietnam achieved the highest level of reading proficiency expected at the end of primary school. The results also show considerable within-country variation in reading proficiency levels (UNICEF and SEAMEO 2020).

In all countries, girls tended to have higher levels of achievement in reading and writing; girls in Cambodia, Malaysia, and the Philippines also demonstrated higher levels of achievement in mathematics. In addition, students from higher

FIGURE 9.3. Proportion of Students in Each Reading Proficiency Level in Grade 5: Southeast Asia Primary Learning Metrics Assessment, 2019

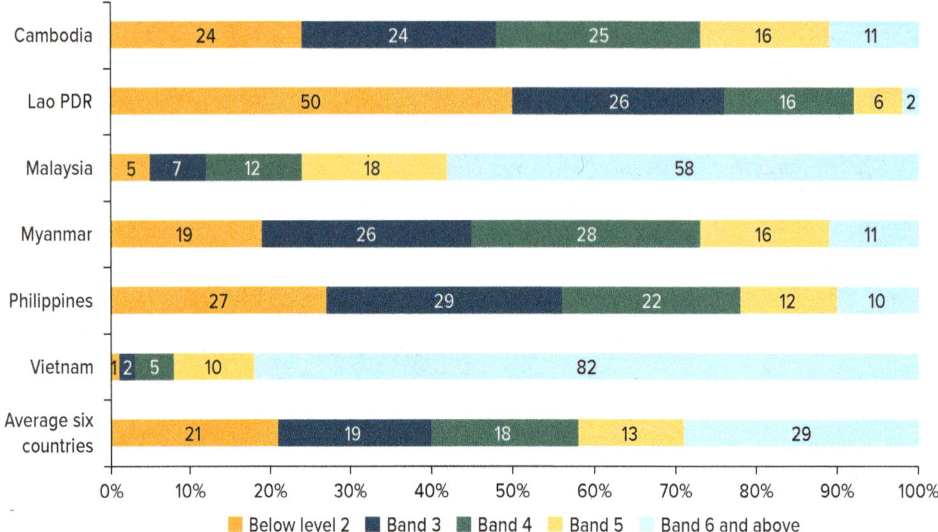

Source: UNICEF and SEAMEO 2020.

socioeconomic backgrounds, students who had attended pre-school, and students who reported using the language of instruction at home all tended to achieve higher reading, writing, and mathematics scores than those who did not fall into these categories (UNICEF and SEAMEO 2020).

References

Amadhila, Leopoldine, Helena Miranda, Sem Shikongo, and Raimo Dengeinge. 2011. "Policy Brief: Quality of Primary School Inputs in Namibia." http://www.sacmeq.org/sites/default/files/sacmeq/reports/sacmeq-iii/policy-brief/nam_school_inputs_15oct2011_final.pdf.

Flotts, Paulina, Jorge Manzi, Daniela Jimenez, Andrea Abarzua, Carlos Cayuman, and Maria José Garcia. 2016. *Informe de Resultados TERCE. Tercer Estudio Regional Comparativo y Explicativo. Logros de Aprendizaje*. Santiago, Chile: OREALC UNESCO.

Greaney, Vincent, and Thomas Kellaghan. 2008. *National Assessments of Educational Achievement, Volume 1: Assessing National Achievement Levels in Education*. Washington, DC: World Bank.

Hungi, Njora, Demus Makuwa, Kenneth Ross, Mioko Saito, Stephanie Dolata, Frank van Capelle, Laura Paviot, and Jocelyne Vellien. 2010. "SACMEQ III Project Results: Pupil Achievement Levels in Reading and Mathematics." http://www.sacmeq.org/sites/default/files/sacmeq/reports/sacmeq-iii/working-documents/wd01_sacmeq_iii_results_pupil_achievement.pdf.

PASEC (Programme d'Analyse des Systèmes Éducatifs de la CONFEMEN). 2015. *PASEC 2014. Education System Performance in Francophone Sub-Saharan Africa. Competencies and Learning Factors in Primary Education*. Dakar, Senegal: PASEC. https://www.pasec.confemen.org/wp-content/uploads/2015/12/Rapport_Pasec2014_GB_webv2.pdf.

SACMEQ (Southern and Eastern Africa Consortium for Monitoring Educational Quality). 2017. "The SACMEQ IV Project in South Africa: A Study of the Conditions of Schooling and the Quality of Education." http://www.sacmeq.org/sites/default/files/sacmeq/publications/sacmeq_iv_project_in_south_africa_report.pdf.

SPC (Pacific Community) and EQAP (Educational Quality and Assessment Programme). 2019. "Pacific Islands Literacy and Numeracy Assessment 2018 Regional Report." Suva, Fiji: SPC. https://research.acer.edu.au/ar_misc/31.

UNICEF (United Nations Children's Fund) and SEAMEO (Southeast Asian Ministers of Education Organization). 2017a. *SEA-PLM 2019 Assessment Framework, 1st Ed.* Bangkok, Thailand: UNICEF and SEAMEO-SEA-PLM Secretariat. https://www.seaplm.org/PUBLICATIONS/frameworks/sea-plm%202019%20assessment%20framework.pdf.

UNICEF (United Nations Children's Fund) and SEAMEO (Southeast Asian Ministers of Education Organization). 2017b. "SEA-PLM 2019 Global Citizenship Assessment Framework, 1st Ed." Bangkok, Thailand: UNICEF and SEAMEO-SEA-PLM Secretariat. https://www.seaplm.org/PUBLICATIONS/frameworks/sea-plm%202019%20global%20citizenship%20assessment%20framework.pdf.

UNICEF (United Nations Children's Fund) and SEAMEO (Southeast Asian Ministers of Education Organization). 2020. *SEA-PLM 2019 Main Regional Report, Children's Learning in 6 Southeast Asian Countries*. Bangkok, Thailand: UNICEF and SEAMEO-SEA-PLM Secretariat.

Regional Assessment Organization Websites

LLECE: https://es.unesco.org/fieldoffice/santiago/projects/llece

PASEC: https://www.pasec.confemen.org

SACMEQ: http://www.sacmeq.org

PILNA: https://eqap.spc.int

SEA-PLM: https://www.seaplm.org

Glossary of Technical Terms

The following definitions have been adapted from the *Standards for Educational and Psychological Testing* (AERA, APA, and NCME 2014) and the *2014 ETS Standards for Quality and Fairness* (ETS 2014).

Accessibility. A test is accessible when its design permits as many students as possible to demonstrate what they know and can do without test or item characteristics that are irrelevant to the knowledge or skill domain being assessed impeding them.

Accommodations. Changes to a test's format or administration conditions to address the needs of particular students (for example, extra testing time for students for whom the language of testing is not the language they speak at home). These changes should not alter the knowledge or skill that the test measures or the ability to compare student scores.

Achievement, proficiency, performance levels. Descriptions of what students know and can do organized into categories on a continuum aligned with content standards (for example, basic, proficient, advanced).

Adaptation, test adaptation. Changes to the original test format or its administration to increase accessibility for students who would otherwise face barriers unrelated to the knowledge domain being assessed; depending on the nature of the adaptation, it may or may not affect test score interpretation. Changes to a test as part of the translation and contextualization process for a particular linguistic and cultural group.

Adaptive test. A test, typically administered on a computer, in which easier or more difficult items are presented depending on a student's correct or incorrect responses to previous items.

Alignment. The degree to which the content and cognitive demands of test items match the targeted content and cognitive demands described in the test specifications.

Alternate assessments, tests. Tests designed to assess the performance of students unable to participate in the regular assessment, even with accommodations. Alternate forms or editions of the same test that measure the same knowledge and skills at the same difficulty level but with different items or tasks.

Comparability, score comparability. The extent to which scores from two or more tests are comparable. The degree of score comparability depends on the type of linking procedure used.

Content standard. A statement of content and skills that students are expected to learn in a subject matter area, often by a particular grade or upon completion of a particular level of schooling.

Criterion-referenced score interpretation. Test score interpretation in relation to a criterion domain. A common example is the use of cut scores and proficiency levels to describe what students with different test scores know and are able to do in a subject area.

Cut score. A point on a score scale above which students are classified differently from those below it. Score interpretation and results reporting differ for students above and below the cut score (for example, pass versus fail, basic versus proficient).

Equating. The statistical process of expressing scores from two or more alternative test forms on a common score scale.

Fairness. A test is fair when any differences in performance between subgroups of students are derived from construct-relevant sources of variance. That is, construct-irrelevant contextual or individual characteristics should not systematically affect test scores that one or more subgroups of students obtain. Group differences in performance do not necessarily make a test unfair, because the groups may differ on the knowledge domain being assessed.

Linking, score linking. Procedure for expressing scores from different tests in a comparable way. Linking methods range from statistical equating to the judgment of subject matter experts.

Norm-referenced score interpretation. Score interpretation based on comparing a student's performance with the score distribution of a reference group (also known as the *norm group*). For instance, a student's score can be described in terms of how far it is from the average for a national sample of students taking the same assessment.

Reliability, precision. The extent to which test scores are free of random measurement error; the likely consistency of the attained test scores across assessment administrations, use of alternative test forms, or scoring by different raters.

Scale score. Transformation of raw test scores into a different metric to facilitate interpretation.

Scaling. Transforming raw test scores to scaled test scores.

Scoring rubric. Established criteria, including rules, principles, and examples, used in scoring open-ended items and performance tasks. The scoring rubric should include rules for and examples of each score level.

Standard-setting. Methods used to determine cut scores on a test and map test scores onto discrete proficiency levels. Normally requires the judgment of subject matter experts and, in some cases, information about test properties and distribution of test scores.

Standardization. Set of procedures and protocols to be followed in the test development and administration process to ensure consistency in testing conditions for all students. Standardization is necessary for fair comparison of test scores of students. Exceptions to standardization may occur when students require accommodations to take the test.

Test specifications. Documentation of the purpose and intended uses of a test and of the test's content, format, length, psychometric characteristics of the items and test overall, delivery mode, administration, scoring, and score reporting.

Universal design. An approach to test development and administration to ensure accessibility of a test to all of its intended students.

Validity. Extent to which interpretations of scores and actions taken on the basis of these scores are appropriate and justified by evidence and theory. Validity refers to how test scores are interpreted and used rather than to the test itself.

Vertical scaling. Procedure to express scores comparably when underlying tests differ in difficulty. Vertical scaling is commonly used to report results from tests administered to students in different grades on the same scale.

References

AERA (American Educational Research Association), APA (American Psychological Association), and NCME (National Council on Measurement in Education). 2014. *Standards for Educational and Psychological Testing*. Washington, DC: AERA.

ETS (Educational Testing Service). 2014. *2014 ETS Standards for Quality and Fairness*. Princeton, NJ: ETS.

ECO-AUDIT

Environmental Benefits Statement

The World Bank Group is committed to reducing its environmental footprint. In support of this commitment, we leverage electronic publishing options and print-on-demand technology, which is located in regional hubs worldwide. Together, these initiatives enable print runs to be lowered and shipping distances decreased, resulting in reduced paper consumption, chemical use, greenhouse gas emissions, and waste.

We follow the recommended standards for paper use set by the Green Press Initiative. The majority of our books are printed on Forest Stewardship Council (FSC)–certified paper, with nearly all containing 50–100 percent recycled content. The recycled fiber in our book paper is either unbleached or bleached using totally chlorine-free (TCF), processed chlorine–free (PCF), or enhanced elemental chlorine–free (EECF) processes.

More information about the Bank's environmental philosophy can be found at http://www.worldbank.org/corporateresponsibility.